THE
FIRE
INSIDE

*A Companion
for the
Creative Life*

LUCY ADKINS AND BECKY BREED

North Carolina

The Fire Inside: A Companion for the Creative Life
© 2021 Lucy Adkins and Becky Breed. All rights reserved.

Published in the United States by WriteLife Publishing
(an imprint of Boutique of Quality Books Publishing Company, Inc.)
www.writelife.com

The poem "Mourning Dove Migration" was previously published in the 2000 Nebraska Poet's Calendar by Black Star Press.

Printed in the United States of America

978-1-60808-248-3 (p)
978-1-60808-249-0 (e)

Library of Congress Control Number 2021931255

Book design by Robin Krauss, www.bookformatters.com
Cover design by Rebecca Lown, www.rebeccalowndesign.com

First editor: Caleb Guard
Second editor: Andrea Vande Vorde

Praise for Lucy Adkins, Becky Breed, and *The Fire Inside*

"Beginning with 'Say Yes to Creativity' and all the way through twelve chapters to 'Just Do It,' *The Fire Inside* is jam-packed with ideas, tips, suggestions, inspiration and general cheering-on. Lucy Adkins and Becky Breed's newest book indeed lights a fire and tells us how to keep the flames burning. Whether using the book as a daily dose of inspiration or a straight-through read (and read again and again), writers and creators of all stripes will be grateful for this lively companion for their life, creative and otherwise."

— Judy Reeves, author of
A Writer's Book of Days and *Wild Women, Wild Voices*

"*The Fire Inside* is packed with stories, lessons, and exercises that encourage readers to grow their creative souls. Written by two empathic educators, this book is practical and passionate, accepting and challenging. It is impossible to read *The Fire Inside* and not be inspired to follow our dreams. I recommend it to all artists and artists to be."

— Mary Pipher, author of
Writing to Change the World and *Women Rowing North*

"A warm and welcome conversation for those searching for their creative identity. Lucy Adkins and Becky Breed offer insights on how to pursue creative passion in the midst of the everyday in order to live a soul-filling, expansive life. Absolutely inspiring."

— Tosca Lee, New York Times bestselling author

"The best books about writing are the ones that don't read like books about writing, but instead feel like conversations with a wise friend who is sitting beside you as you write, encouraging and guiding you every step of the way. That is the kind of book Adkins and Breed have written, again. Like their first book, *Writing in Community: Say Goodbye to Writer's Block and Transform Your Life*, this book, *The Fire Inside*, is sure to find a space on the shelf nearest your favorite writing spot and will become one of the most dog-eared books on that shelf. There is inspiration on every page."

– Karen Gettert Shoemaker, author of *The Meaning of Names*

"If ever there was a book that could help the aspiring creative past the fear of finding and exercising the creative potential that stirs within all beings, it is this book: *The Fire Inside: A Companion for the Creative Life*. And a faithful companion it is. Lucy Adkins and Becky Breed have written a book that invites us to come forward with such intelligence and grace as to be irresistible. On every page they speak to the creative process and the creative spirit with a clarity that allows the reader to recognize the fire inside and believe in it as rightfully theirs. If you bring this wonderful book home, and hold it close, you will never walk alone in the vast field that is creative living."

– Philip Kenney, author of *The Writer's Crucible*

"A fine companion for anyone looking to begin or deepen a creative life. Filled with practical advice on getting started, nurturing inspiration, and connecting with other seekers in your community, *The Fire Inside* offers meditative and effective writing prompts that will help you observe the world and yourself in a more significant way."

– Theodore Wheeler, author of *In Our Other Lives*

Table of Contents

Introduction

The underlying principle of *The Fire Inside* is that, whether we recognize it or not, we are all inherently creative, though creativity doesn't happen in isolation. It happens when we open ourselves to possibility, to the idea that we create not only out of our innermost beings, our unique selves, but in partnership with mystery, the life-giving source that helps us achieve what is latent inside.

The ideas presented within these pages grew out of many years of devoting ourselves to the practice of creativity, working by ourselves and with others, paying attention to the process, and wanting to share what we have learned. We've learned how to find our rhythms, let go of what holds us back, woo the muse, and make the "magic" happen more often. We learned that when we do, the tremendous power of creativity fills our lives with purpose, cultivates opportunity, and connects us to the rest of the world in ways we would never imagine.

Our first book, *Writing in Community: Say Goodbye to Writer's Block and Transform Your Life,* examined the potential of inspiration and connection within a writing community, how we can find our authentic voices working shoulder to shoulder with other writers. In this book, we take the process a step further, combining one hundred and twenty personal narratives and essays along with questions for reflection to explore how each individual can grow in their creative lives. It describes the cyclical nature of creativity—the times we need to persist as well as the times we need to let go, when we need to re-energize ourselves by exploring new places, new types of creativity, and seeking out and nurturing relationships with mentors. And it describes the times we would benefit from being in solitude, keeping company with ourselves in a quiet place.

We learned, and learned again, that great effort and patience are required, that we will experience delays and frustrations. But how much clay must we fire to create the pot we envision? How many pages of a short story must we shred before we craft the satisfying, mesmerizing end? Gratification has its own timetable. But when it arrives—when a ballet dancer performs a successful dance series, when the book of poetry is published, the delight is incomparable.

When you live your creativity, it's an amazing journey. We want this book to be a companion on the way, to encourage and inspire you, and provide gentle proddings to help you continue the creative work you love. We craft our lives from the fire inside—listening to the spirit and following the promptings of the heart. Let them be amazing.

Authors' Note

The examples and stories within these pages are the truth as we have experienced it through writing, study, participating in various writing and creative communities, and living in this world. Some of the names have been changed for purposes of confidentiality.

PART ONE:
THE INVITATION

The place God calls you to is the place where your deep gladness and the world's deep hunger meet.

—Frederick Buechner, *Wishful Thinking*

Chapter One:
Say "Yes" to Creativity

The Fire Inside

Inner fire is the most important thing we possess.

—Edith Södergran, *The Poet who Created Herself:*
The Complete Letters of Edith Södergran
to Hagar Olsson

Deep within us, we have a yearning, a passion, a desire to make and to do, to create something out of our hearts and imaginations that did not exist before. To bring forth something new upon the earth. It is innate in us, this intense wanting, and when we are engaged in the specific type of creativity we were meant to do—whether it be painting, writing, making music, or designing a new way to educate our children—we experience what Martha Graham calls "a vitality, a life force, an energy, a quickening."[1] It's what puts the spark in our eyes, the skip in our steps. It is the fire inside.

Do you know that fire? Sometimes it manifests itself as restlessness, a vague dissatisfaction, a feeling that there is something important you must do, you *have* to do, to be true to yourself. It is the little ache you feel when you read a story that is heartbreakingly true and think *I want to do that*, or when you see a painting that stuns you with its power, and your fingers itch to pick up a paintbrush. Maybe it isn't exactly clear what is burning inside, what you want and are put on earth to do.

---

[1] Agnes DeMille, *Martha: The Life and Work of Martha Graham* (New York: Random House, 1991), 264.

3

The Fire Inside

Or perhaps you know in your bones that you must write poetry, you must dance or die, you must create gardens of incredible beauty, but maybe you're afraid that if you try you will fall flat on your face. You doubt yourself and your abilities.

This is the way we humans are, having an intense wanting on one hand, fear and doubt on the other. But let us accept as an essential truth that we are all creative, wildly creative, each and every one of us—that we have vast reserves of untapped talents and abilities—songs only we can write, sculptures waiting to be born from the unique spirit that is us; and when we accept that belief and act on it, oh, then! We wake each day with a new animation, a vibrancy and passion. We feel like children let out of a stuffy classroom into a blue-sky spring day, and we can't wait to see what we can do with it.

The fire inside is the "something" that fascinates you, intrigues you, so that you go to sleep and wake up thinking about it. You want to study it from all its interesting angles and make it central to your life, keep working at it, falling short in your aspirations at times, but trying and trying again. And if you are not currently involved with something that brings with it such zeal, if you've kept your fire tamped down, unable to act on your passion for whatever reason, know that it is still there—the beginning of days filled with intense purpose and meaning, waiting for you.

The Highest Kite

Imagination is the highest kite that can fly.
—Lauren Bacall, *By Myself and Then Some*

The human brain is a remarkable thing. It keeps the body going, stores knowledge, analyzes, remembers, puts two and two together to make sense of the world, and somehow allows for the miracle of imagination. When we were children, we lived in worlds rich in imagination, allowing us to transform a blanket draped over a chair into a cave, the tree-filled ditch behind the house into a secret forest. We carried out endless adventures in the worlds we created, the synapses in our brains sparking with delight and excitement.

But when we become adults and take on duty and responsibility, we don't invite imagination out to play as much as we used to. The good news—especially for those wanting to live more creative lives—is that we can become just as involved in flights of fancy as we used to be, rediscovering the world in all its beauty, its design as well as its asymmetrical magnificence. Ask yourself: if you were a little seed in the ground waiting for spring to warm you and pull the green living-ness of you up to the sun, what would that be like? If you were a baby robin in a blue egg in a nest, how would it be pecking your way into the world? Crazy questions, maybe, but ones that can stimulate us to bursts of creativity, and as Lauren Bacall suggests, that is a joyous way of living in this world.

So, if you haven't exercised the muscles of your imagination lately, why not start now? Not that you have to embark on a novel, necessarily, or begin work on the next Mona Lisa; you can begin simply and joyfully as children do. Look at pictures of art and imagine stepping inside the frames. Who would you talk to and what would you see? Or look outside your window and take note of the different elements there. Maybe you see a bird flying or tree branches swaying in the breeze, then imagine a conversation with that bird or that tree.

It may come haltingly at first, in fits and starts, but when you let whimsy back into your life, the brain begins to work in new ways, mapping out new neural pathways. And like muscles gradually becoming stronger as you exercise, so does the imagination become livelier and more free-wheeling. You will find your life opening up, becoming richer as your mind discovers ideas for your next artistic project in the pattern of the night sky or the sound of the wind before a storm. Imagination can be the be-all and end-all for you; it can be everything.

Late Bloomers

We always may be what we might have been.

—Adelaide Anne Procter,
The Ghost in the Picture Room

I didn't start to write seriously until I was in my mid-forties, and although I was overjoyed to (finally) discover what I truly loved, from time to time I find myself with a bad case of the "If Onlys." If only I'd started writing earlier . . . if only I'd taken creative writing in college . . .

When my mind starts to go in that direction, I like to think about people like Grandma Moses, who didn't take up painting until her late seventies, and then went on to astound the world. Or Laura Ingalls Wilder, who published the first of her many books at age sixty-four. There are other "late bloomers" like this, people like Julia Child, whose first cookbook came into print when she was forty-nine and David Sedaris, author of *Me Talk Pretty One Day*, who debuted on NPR at age forty-four. Their accomplishments did not come until later in life, but they *did come*—and for those of us who are men or women of a certain age and concerned about the time we have left to achieve our creative dreams, this is encouraging.

Why is it that some artists and writers—geniuses like Mozart and Picasso—find success early on in their lives, and others not until much later? University of Chicago economist David Galenson theorizes that the timing of an individual's success lies in the artist's *approach* to their art—whether they start out with a clear idea of the *concept* they are after, or whether it's more about the *journey*.

For many of us, the reason our creative successes take place later in life may be much simpler. We started late, not seriously beginning to pursue our creative passions until our forties or fifties or sixties—or even later. This might happen for several reasons:

- We didn't *find* our passions until later in life.

- We were discouraged in our early efforts—discouraged by parents, teachers, or friends. Discouraged even by ourselves, thinking that our dream was too frivolous, too hard, or that we lacked talent.

- We didn't have sufficient financial resources to attain the education and training we needed, and it was necessary to spend the majority of our time making a living.

- We needed to devote our energies and time to raising a family.

Whatever the reason, late bloomers like Grandma Moses, David Sedaris, and others provide hope that whatever age we are, it's not too late. Not too late to learn to paint, to play a musical instrument, or to try your hand at writing.

Small Beginnings

Big things have small beginnings.
—Peter O'Toole, *Lawrence of Arabia*

We are encouraged to think big, to dream big, and that is good advice. We as individuals are capable of great and many accomplishments, and our vision should be as large and limitless as our possibilities. *But it is important, also, to think small.* Not in regards to our potential, but in regards to the steps needed to reach that potential. "You need to be content with small steps," Katie Kacvinsky wrote. "That's all life is. Small steps that you take every day so when you look back down the road it all adds up and you know you have covered some distance."[2]

When recovering from a virus or a bad case of the flu, something that truly gets you down, it may be that you've rallied to the extent that the debilitating headache and fever are gone, but still, you're weak. It's frustrating. Seeing all you want and need to do but not feeling well enough to dive back into your routine. So you do what you can. A writer friend shared with me her process of getting back to full-strength after an illness. She writes a paragraph—then goes back to the couch to rest. Twenty minutes later, she may get up and make some Jell-O, then rests again, repeating the process as long as she feels able. And while she's not a ball of fire, (as she says) launching into her work with great gusto, she's still getting something done, making headway.

Twenty some years ago, I took a novel writing workshop. Writing a novel had always been a mysterious and wonderful something calling out to me—*come and write me.* But an entire novel? Three hundred

---

[2] Katie Kacvinsky, *Awaken* (New York: Houghton Mifflin Harcourt Publishing Company, 2011), 272.

or so pages of a book? It was daunting, seemingly impossible. The instructor, however, said something I'll never forget: that a novel is just one scene, and then another, and another until the book is completed, the story told.

Of course that's true, but hearing it laid out simply as she did, making the project a series of small, manageable tasks made it something doable. Since that time, I've completed quite a few projects that way—everything from writing and editing a novel to accomplishing at least something in a day when I'm not feeling the best. "Success is the sum of small efforts, repeated day in and day out," Robert Collier said. Mother Theresa suggests we "do small things with great love." The little things *do* make a difference, as our mothers told us. We can create a life that way.

We may find ourselves speaking disparagingly of our talents. We say that the poems we write are really nothing special, the sketches in our notebooks just a little thing we do. Yet if we search our inner selves deeply enough, we realize that we are like children pulling at our teachers' sleeves, wanting them to see us, to recognize the spark beneath the words we write, the emotional pull in the sketches. It's there, if we dare admit it, the flicker of what may grow to be fabulous, latent but powerful. And little by little, as we take on the assignments presented to us, as we keep working, small accomplishments turn into bigger ones, and our dreams edge ever closer.

Is Something Missing?

People who follow their joy . . . discover a depth of
creativity and talent that inspires us.

—Robert Holden, *Follow Your Joy*

Have you felt it? A feeling of emptiness at times, an ambiguous longing, a sense that time is passing and you're missing out on something? It's a common enough feeling. Too often, we put our creative selves on hold, allowing our traditional roles as men and women to dominate our lives. Every day we go about our tasks, doing the best we can to be diligent, hardworking employees, parents who do the right things, and people always on call for others. But how do we prevent our jobs from eating up our time? Where do we draw the line regarding obligations to family and friends?

We can't do it all. Still we try, the tug of overwhelming expectations pulling in so many directions that we forget what stirs us, what brings authenticity and new energy to our lives. We *can,* however, reawaken our creativity, fall in love again with that part of ourselves which gives us meaning and joy. How do we do this?

First of all, we have to notice something is missing; and, for many of us, the process of awakening is similar to what happens when we choose to ignore a dripping faucet. Drip after drip, day after day, we pay no attention. Then one morning, water suddenly gushes out in a tremendous stream—we can't stop its pouring forth—and we have to admit we've had a problem for a long time. In the same way, going about our daily lives, the unexpected occurs—an injury, the loss of a job, some other startling occurrence—and we're caught off-guard, jolted awake, recognizing that we're not living our lives as we've intended. That we ourselves seem to be less than before, diminished,

11

doing this or that only out of a sense of duty or habit, our personal hopes and dreams nowhere in sight.

My friend Ellie had an experience like that, one that changed the course of her life. Besides being the primary caretaker for five children, Ellie loved to draw, to express herself through pen and ink, pencil and charcoal, and found it maddening that others defined her only as a wife and mother. Furthermore, she realized she'd allowed that to happen, ignoring the urgings of her soul, forgetting herself who *she* was.

Then, one night, rising from bed to check on a sick child, she was startled by moonlight streaming through the window, beautiful, glorious, reaching into every corner, it seemed, so that the room was suffused with gold. She was overcome with awe, taken aback. That gold came night after night, of course it did, but lately, she hadn't noticed it. Her hands started to tingle, and she knew then she couldn't return to bed. Instead, for the first time in months, she rushed to her workroom, gathered pencils and charcoal, took out her drawing paper, and began to sketch out what she'd experienced: those touches of gold, that awakening, the essence of miracles that are all around us.

We don't have to wait for a roomful of golden light to get our attention, but we do have to recognize what's missing in our lives. The next time a cardinal comes to your window, or you're drinking your favorite green tea, ask yourself: *Am I making room for joy in my life? For that which brings about contentment and bliss, and expresses the creative me?* If not, turn your attention to finding the things for which you are grateful. With gratitude comes joy, which leads to bringing more creativity into our lives—and in turn, new moments of joy, the potential going on and on.

The Secret Garden

The earth has music for those who listen.
—Reginald Holmes, *The Magic of Sound*

There is a story of a spoiled and lonely young girl trying to make a new life after the death of her parents. Do you know it? It is *The Secret Garden*, a classic children's book I didn't discover until I was an adult, when it pulled at me, reached into me, maybe because its appeal is universal. For aren't we all spoiled a little (at least as compared to most of the world)? And aren't we all lonely and searching?

The little girl, Mary, is sent to her uncle's home on the moors of England, where, bored and unhappy, she wanders outside in the cold of early spring, and behind an ivy-covered wall, discovers a hidden garden. She is intrigued—here is something new—but the gray and brown tendrils of climbing roses, the foliage of plants beneath her feet, appear dry and lifeless. The garden she has found is dead. Still, Mary is a curious sort, and when she picks up a stick and begins to scratch in the soil, she discovers the green poking up points of crocuses and jonquils struggling to the light.

This is thrilling, the unseen potential, the inherent possibility that exists within the earth, the inherent possibility that lives within *us*. For we all have little sprouts of watercolors or mosaics or songs waiting to arise out of our beings, and bring new beauty to the world.

Sometimes it seems that we have nothing new to offer—no ideas, no inspiration—but like Mary, if we poke around a little, if we put our pens to paper or pick up a paintbrush and start to fiddle about, some spark in us ignites, and we begin to work. Maybe we are inspired to create custom gold-edged wedding cakes decorated with flowers, or make art from the doorknobs and hinges found in old farmhouses.

The Fire Inside

Whatever it may be, it is as if some essence in the words or the materials we are using becomes energized, as if what we are making *wants* to come into being. It takes hold of us, uses us, and is created.

In *The Secret Garden,* Mary returns every day to the hidden place behind the ivy-covered wall. She clears a space around each bit of green she finds and places seeds in the soil. And as she works, a little every day, the garden comes alive. It can be that way for us, too, when we find space in our lives for our creativity, and when we work steadily and faithfully. Then, brushstroke by brushstroke, the paintings will come, and line by line, the poems.

Those Places We Call Home

I am rooted, but I flow.

—Virginia Woolf, *The Waves*

Oh, those places we once called home: a farmhouse on the plains, a two-story brick house in Baltimore—a little old-fashioned, perhaps a little run-down—but places where we were comfortable in our skins, where we were understood and loved. They may be gone from us now, but still they beckon and shimmer before our eyes like mirages in the desert. How deeply they hold our imaginations, burning within in a slow smoldering pitch; and what staying power they have in our psyches, inextricably tied to our dreams. We long for them, for what we've lost; or perhaps this holds more truth: we yearn for the dream that could have been.

Sometimes we feel life has a certain inevitability, that we're on a course we can't get off, a trajectory which does not speak to who we are. But that can change. When we absorb ourselves in creating art, we find home—the deepest part of ourselves where we give life and form to our dreams, where we shape how we perceive the world we live in. Where's home? Home is a place where we are most grounded and where all the threads of who we are exist together. Perhaps more than anything, home is where we find our truest selves.

Making art gives us the chance to plumb our own depths, connect with what steadies and reassures us. Reaching deep inside to touch the currents of our lives, we make lived experiences what we want. Our pieces radiate the essence of who we are from the deepest caverns of our beings and illuminate to us previously unimaginable, beautiful futures. Even with the disappointments that come inevitably with being alive, we still have tangible expressions of our creativity.

The Fire Inside

All art has the potential of changing us, as poetry helps us get at the heart of our experiences, calling forth a deeper self. Poetry begins with a wanting, an intense longing, something like a homesickness, an ache deep inside. Isn't that one of the reasons we turn to our easels, go to our pottery wheels? That homesickness? Knowing that faithfulness to our art will take us where we need to be.

Everyday Creativity

*You can't use up creativity. The more you use, the more
you have.*

—Maya Angelou, *Bell Telephone Magazine*

Bill and Stephanie were remodeling, trying to spruce up the bathroom
in their sixty-five-year-old house without breaking the bank. One of
the problems was the medicine cabinet, caked with layers of paint,
rust eating away at the shelves. But its frame and overall design were
charming, a kind of French "shabby chic," with an overemphasis,
lately, on the "shabby." Bill opted for refurbishing, and after removing
the cabinet from the wall and spending weekends painting, sanding,
and repainting, he completed the job. The cabinet was clean and fresh
again, its simple elegance restored. Still, all was not perfect. When
refitted back into its opening, the cabinet door wouldn't close, leaving
a gap. Not a very big gap, but a gap nonetheless.

After a week or two of thinking this might be something they'd just
need to learn to live with, Bill came home from a conference with an
idea. He removed the magnetic closure from his conference nametag,
attached it to the inside of the cabinet door, and *voila!* The door closed
with a satisfying click. This is creativity in action, everyday creativity,
that we all possess and often fail to recognize.

When we think about creative people, we think of the Toni
Morrisons of the world, the Dorothea Langes, and Pablo Picassos. It
is an ethereal plane they reside on, we believe—a place inaccessible
to most. But though it may be argued that these people represent the
upper echelons of creativity, there *is* room for us.

Our grandparents and great-aunts and uncles of the Depression era
may very well have been the most creative people we've ever known,

using the odd bolt and baling wire to repair the windmill or the screen door, mixing this or that from the pantry into previously-unheard-of meal combinations when supplies ran low. They got creative. They would have said they "made do," as others of the time did, their creative spirit coming about by necessity. From scarcity, from lack.

Creativity is about flexibility, adaptability, seeing new uses for what is around us. It is moving into a drab apartment and refusing to accept drab as your fate, deciding instead to add a splash of bright color on a wall, find a classy "antique" rocker at Goodwill.

We are all creative in many ways—in the manner we dress: choosing feather or shell earrings, pairing different pants and tops, using a scarf for a belt. We find innovative means of stretching the budget, keeping the lawn mower or the car going a little longer. One friend creates picnic tables from wooden spools that once held rolls of cable, another melts down the stub ends of candles and drizzles them over pinecones for fire starters.

Our creativity quotients are greater than we know. Not only can everyday creativity add beauty to the world, solve problems, and save money, it's invigorating. You earn the right to walk around for a while with a smug smile on your face. And in a world where there is much to put you down, you feel imaginative, resourceful; you feel good about yourself. The little spark in you flares into life. It *is* there, and since creativity breeds more creativity, who knows what your amazing imagination will dream up next?

What's Your Life Assignment?

You were put on earth to achieve your greatest self, to live out your purpose, and do it courageously.
—Steve Maraboli, *Life, The Truth, and Being Free*

One Saturday morning, I was running errands when I heard a message I'll never forget. The car radio was tuned to a talk-interview program and a woman's voice came through the speakers, deep and powerful, reverberating through the car like a clap of thunder. "You've got to find your passion," she said. "Your life assignment." Life assignment? I almost went through a red light.

"You may avoid it, put it off—but deep down inside, you know what your assignment is." A car honked from behind—the light had turned green, and I drove on, dazzled and amazed. It was almost as if the voice were speaking directly to *me*. For weeks afterwards, I kept thinking about what I'd heard. What *was* my passion, my purpose in life, my life assignment?

Each of us is uniquely different—each with a special kind of light: perhaps the ability to see through problems and find an answer, or to create beauty through music, art, or making a beautiful home. We may have gifts in technical and mechanical areas, or the gift of comforting, of knowing and saying the right thing—and many others beyond these. Sometimes our gifts are obvious. We may be gifted in cooking or balancing a budget, and we recognize those. At other times we have to search deeper within and ask: *What excites me? If time and money weren't a factor, what would I like to do?* Learn to paint? Play the piano?

The thing is, we have many gifts, and as our lives go on, we continue developing the ones we recognize, and discovering more.

And with each of these gifts comes an assignment—to use them for the betterment of ourselves and those around us.

Too many times, however, we ignore or discount the ear we have for music, the ability to inspire others, and do nothing to develop these abilities further. But when we take on the assignments presented to us, when we live out our passions—what we were meant to do and be—then life gets exciting. Perhaps your ear for music leads you to discovering an aptitude for the piano, which steers you to Rockabilly and the blues, then a fascination with the music of Nina Simone and Norah Jones. You play and sing with your whole body, your whole heart, and begin organizing jam sessions, sharing your passion with others, turning their lives as well as yours in new and amazing directions. We never know where a seemingly small gift or passion may take us unless we explore it. This is living a life with purpose; this is living well.

The Wild Silky Part

Who knows anyway what it is, that wild, silky part of
ourselves without which no poem can live?

—Mary Oliver, *A Poetry Handbook*

What is it that gives us the ability to create art, the part of us that shimmers inside, that makes our skin tingle when we select a certain word for a poem and know it is right? Is it some ancestral knowledge stockpiled in our DNA? The slender thread that connects us to the divine? Whatever it is, this wild silkiness is a shy little thing. It makes its appearance in quick flashes, then disappears, somewhere out of reach. Still we know it is out there, that marvelous and mysterious "something," and until it comes again, we feel a little lost, incomplete.

In Celtic and Scandinavian folklore, parents passed on to their children stories about certain "seal people" who could remove their seal skins, take human form, and walk on two legs on land. And when they yearned again for the sea, they'd slip back into their skins and return to the water. In human form, these "selkies" or "silkies" are portrayed as beautiful people with large seal eyes. Kind, gentle people who suffered living dual lives, yearning for the land when living as seals, and missing their seal families while on shore.

Most likely, Mary Oliver wasn't referring to the mythological silkies when she wrote of the "wild silky" part that exists within each of us. But it is apt to think of the heart of our creativity in that way. It's slippery and elusive, the way it is when we are searching for love. We long for a certain someone who is the other half of ourselves, who can make us whole, in just the way we long to capture a certain feeling in the landscape we're painting, or the quirky but just right idea for our next collage. We feel in our bones that the person we love is out there.

21

And we sense with an out-of-body feeling that the idea is out there, too—intangible, hidden in the shadows, but there. Like a dream we knew we had but can't quite remember.

Perhaps that is the wild, silky part of who we are, the God part, the part that knows innately the soul of a work of art. And if only we can slip into our sealskins and return to the water, we will remember the dream, discover what we need to do to seize upon that feeling for our painting, the idea for our novel. We know it is possible and when we find it, it will be wonderful, like love.

For Your Journey

Many times we are held back from pursuing our creative dreams by fear that others might think our yearnings foolish. So we keep them hidden. We keep them to ourselves. Still, we recognize in our truest selves an inner longing to write or to sing, or perhaps a desire to paint or take lessons in modern dance. Inside each of us are latent abilities, talents upon talents just waiting to be unleashed. And when we open ourselves to allow these possibilities, we will bloom as we never imagined.

1. Open your notebook and jot down the following phrase, completing the blank with what you would like to try, or spend more time doing.

   I would love to try or spend more time _____

   Rewrite the phrase and complete each blank at least four more times. Next, choose two of the items from your list and for each, think of a small step you could take to begin spending time at what you love. If you would like to try your hand at garden design, you might check out a landscaping book from the library. If you would like to try modern dance, research two or three dance studios in your area. Small steps, yes, but important beginnings.

2. Each of us was put on this earth with certain innate talents and abilities, things we were meant to do. Some of us can identify almost immediately what these might be, what is "calling" to us. For others of us, it may take a little time. The best way to do so is to follow the love trail. What do you love? What

puts the shine in your eyes? (And there will be more than one thing.) Find some meditation time, some time alone, and consider what you love, what might be calling to you. Maybe it is spending time messing with watercolors, or taking pictures and arranging them in a scrapbook to tell a story. Maybe you love figuring out the plots in mystery novels. Jot these down in your notebook. Try this exercise several times a week, several times a month. You'll begin to see patterns and themes and it may become clearer what you love to do.

3. Every day we are presented with many choices—to say "yes" or "no" to new experiences. The piano sits in a corner, but we are busy and pass it by, saying no to the new song we could learn, the tune that's been drifting in and out of our minds. We look into our closets and say no to the dance outfit, the denim paint-spattered shirt we use when playing with ceramics or watercolors. We may be used to saying no, sticking to the tried and true.

Take a day to be more consciously alert to the choices you make, and look for opportunities to say "yes" more often to that which can enrich your life. "Yes" to new experiences, new adventures, "yes" to deepening your life.

Chapter Two:
How Creativity Nurtures

Seek Wholeness

We are whole creatures in potential, and the true purpose of desire is to unfold that wholeness, to become what we can be.

—Eric Butterworth, *Spiritual Economics*

When our outside lives drop away, what defines the artist? The electrifying force of creativity. A force that sweeps away boredom, recalibrates our experiences, and leaves delight in its wake. "Follow Your Bliss," Joseph Campbell wrote, and if you do, "you put yourself on a kind of a track that has been there all the while, waiting for you, and the life you ought to be living."[3] Isn't that what we want? The time and space to do what we were put on earth to do? To empty ourselves of the world's distractions—the emails and errands, the endless social obligations that leave us feeling hollow—empty ourselves of all this and allow what waits for us to reveal itself? It's like stepping outside yourself and listening to the whisperings of your innermost voice.

What *is* your bliss? And how will you know when it appears? It's when we connect to what matters, what sings in our hearts. When we become open to the person inside, what we were born to do, and when we find it, we say: *Yes! That's what I want.* We are constantly being fed experiences as to what our wholeness might be, our daily

---

[3] Joseph Campbell, *The Power of Myth* (New York: Anchor Books, 1988) 113.

encounters holding a set of choices pointing us either toward or away from our destinies, but we must choose wisely. Learn to trust in our talents and in the essence of who we are as creative beings. The work is yours, Campbell said. "You have to learn to recognize your own depth."[4]

For all of us on the way to becoming whole, it is as if the path lies in darkness. We search and quest, remaining open until something rises before us. Maybe formed as the lofty star of hope. Sometimes materializing in the raw, undiluted nature of inspiration. You may see shadowy outlines or hear the soft murmur of voices beckoning to you. A sense of great wonder and release follows, and the emergence of what is to be becomes clearer and clearer.

When we bring our attention, passion, and curiosity to a place of rest, we gradually uncover what we are wired to do. And then we begin to love that place, to understand that we find our bliss when we express without hesitation our needs and desires, and ultimately, when we find gladness in what we create.

---

[4] Ibid, 147.

Happiness/Sadness

Even a happy life cannot be without a measure of darkness, and the word happy would lose its meaning if it were not balanced by sadness.

—Carl Jung, from *The Art of Living*

Happiness and sadness are all mixed up in this life. You are passed over for a promotion and come home from work determined to wallow in despair, but your silly-minded dog has other ideas. A beloved brother-in-law dies tragically and too young, and is buried on one of the most beautiful fall days you have ever known. In the midst of death, life insists upon itself. How can we explain this?

Recently, our writing group tackled this enigma of joy in the midst of sorrow, writing from an exercise my friend Barbara suggested. We started out by reading Natalie Goldberg's great poem, "Top of My Lungs," about finding delight in the midst of hard times. First we made a list of some of the sadnesses we have known, then turned abruptly and began writing about times we were outrageously happy.

Oh, the pieces we wrote that night! Dee wrote about New Mexico, a place where she had once lived and still loved, and how she might never be able to visit again; Leo wrote about being in Basic Training—the potato peeling, endless marching, the merciless, red-faced sergeant who breathed down his neck; and Heidi wrote about the terrors of stage fright at an open mic reading. These were wonderful writings, full of the poignancy and pain of living. We laughed out loud at the hilarity of life and felt the tug in our midsections as pain was relived.

It's difficult to explain and to understand why happiness and sadness are so inextricably intertwined. Maybe it is from the dizzying heights of joy that we can best see how sorrow might be waiting, and

27

realize that happiness would have no meaning but for its counterpart of despair. It is in times that we are raw with emotion, when we feel most keenly, that we turn to art. "God is in the sadness and the laughter," Neale Donald Walsch said, "the bitter and the sweet."[5] This is the stuff of life from which we create sculpture or poetry or music, translating deep emotion into beauty.

[5] Neale Donald Walsch, *Conversations With God* (New York: Penguin Putnam Inc., 1995) 60.

Accumulate Riches

I'm a poet. Oh, I'm independently wealthy.
—David Whyte, *Dumbo Feather Magazine*

Once we begin to nurture our creative selves and live the life of the imagination, we discover that along with developing our talents, we become rich, perhaps rich in ways we've never considered. As artists, we surround ourselves with the luxuries of the world, with that which brings pleasure to the senses—the feel of clay beneath our fingertips, the textures of silk or wool, the lavish exuberance of the colors—red, aquamarine, yellow in all its varying shades. We immerse ourselves in music, its staccatos and diminuendos. And for writers, there is the great luxuriance of words. All of which lifts us, which touches our souls and makes us rich. There is something in us that needs beauty. We hunger for it; and when we are engrossed in our art day after day, we encounter that beauty and bask in it.

Artists and writers have the opportunity of seeing the world, seeing *ourselves,* in bigger, more compassionate ways. As we do in writing poetry. As we do in creating plotlines that resonate with the complexities of living in this world, involving ourselves with characters who reflect not only the imperfections of humanity but also our moments of grace. Maybe the protagonist in your short story is willful, a little full of herself sometimes, but when a friend is threatened, faces down a bully. Or you write a poem about a harried young mother in a supermarket shouting at her child, then bursting into tears at what she has done. Perhaps from time to time, *you* have been a little full of yourself; perhaps *you* have been that young mother; and so you write that poem, that short story with great generosity and understanding.

Then there is the gift of resilience, the sweat equity earned in cultivating our art, the persistence we develop. When we write of other people's writing struggles, it is code for *our* struggles. Our endeavors range from frustration to exhilaration; sometimes we feel like we're hitting our heads against a brick wall, but we keep on, determined. Maybe it is that way for you, too. We are tenacious, and with that tenacity over a period of time, we learn, we grow, and develop a sense of mastery and accomplishment.

Our greatest wealth, we know, lies not in our bank accounts or stock portfolios but in lives well lived, in satisfying the yearnings of our souls. We don't want to be starving artists in freezing garrets in Paris. (Well, maybe we want Paris.) But we want more than Maseratis or luxury dwellings and over-the-top lifestyles. Let us go over the top with what is fulfilling, the fruit of our imaginings as evidenced in a sequence of wall hangings we've designed and completed, a new song composed and played so beautifully it brings tears to the eyes. Above all, let's go overboard with the contentment of spending long hours doing what we love. This is wealth beyond any other.

Creativity, the Soft Edge of Grief

Grief is in two parts. The first is loss. The second is the
remaking of life.

—Ann Rolphe, *Bridge of Life Newsletter*

Grief changes us. It forces us to be larger, large enough to hold all the
hurt and sadness of loss. It asks us to hold the ragged love felt in our
bodies and minds for what we once had that is now gone. When we
grieve, the raw centers of our beliefs and attitudes about life are laid
bare, and we question our limits of understanding.

As painful as it may be, it's important to hold on to grief for a time,
hang out with it and let it move through you, much as creativity does.
Allow it to give rise to whatever is there, and when you're ready to
take that first step to healing, know that art will sustain you. Even at
your lowest, even in the depths of despair, it's possible to experience
growth and transformation. To re-imagine your life and discover how
to shape a different future, perhaps even create a new identity. Re-
imagining involves creativity. It softens the edge of grief by offering
the gift of a new beginning, an opportunity to be re-invigorated and to
remake your life. You'll find yourself doing things you never would
have dreamed.

Waking up with grief is like waking up with not enough air. We
choke, remembering, recognizing that in addition to our huge losses,
our lives are full of small disappointments as well, sadnesses that
pierce us to the bone. How does the heart hold all this? My friend
Kim expresses these complex feelings through intricate stained-glass
creations, heart-shaped designs fashioned with holes, empty spaces
that represent the depth and contours of loss over a lifetime. Moving

from a favorite school, being turned down for a promotion, the passing of a much-loved grandmother.

Artists and writers have long used adversity as pathways to creativity. In adapting to sorrow, we find new voices and become more resourceful, more motivated. After the death of her husband, my neighbor and talented friend, Rosanne, wrote a daily blog for a year and shared it with hundreds on Facebook. The writing helped her heal, and in the process, revealed a person highly introspective and unafraid to go where her heart beckoned. Later, she published a book based on these writings to help others overcome their grief and find new lives. Our heart's bliss and our suffering are inextricably linked.

Ron, a lover of music and a gifted musician, unexpectedly lost his wife and companion of many years. And in the soul-numbing months afterwards, he worked with a luthier to create a custom-made guitar in her honor, a guitar that would (as he told me) "bring smiles and joy to all those who see it and hear it for the next hundred years." It was made of light-red walnut, reminiscent of Laura's flowing, auburn hair; and as Ireland was her favorite place, featured mother-of-pearl inlays with a Celtic theme. Besides being a fitting tribute, whenever he plays, it's a way of keeping her alive.

Allowing our creativity to lead us through dark times—whether we are splashing paints on canvas, planting flower seeds after winter's thaw, or throwing clay on a wheel—we begin to feel differently. It's like we've been walking on thin ice for a while and then, ever so slowly, firm ground forms beneath our feet.

Writing the Secrets

When we deny our stories and disengage from tough emotions, they don't go away; instead, they own us, they define us. Our job is not to deny the story, but to defy the ending—to rise strong, recognize our story, and rumble with the truth until we get to a place where we think, Yes. This is what happened. This is my truth. And I will choose how this story ends.

—Brené Brown, *Rising Strong*

Willa Cather wrote about the double life that exists in families: the group life and the one underneath that is "secret, and passionate and intense." The latter one she calls the *real* life which can exist between a loving husband and wife, adoring sisters, or children and their grandparents. In these relationships, Cather continued, " . . . there are innumerable shades of sweetness and anguish."[6]

We all have secrets: some big, and some small. These secrets may be sweet—the first kiss with a boy in sixth grade, or the thrill of sneaking out during all-night slumber parties. There are other secrets, however, that we keep under wraps. They're like the skin beneath a scab: tender, not quite healed. We keep them hidden away as long as we can cover them with a Band-Aid of disguise, telling ourselves they do not have a future, only a connection to the past. Still, they keep coming back, tormenting us like the incessant ticking of a loud clock. Secrets like when Grandma got sick.

The day remembered was the kind of spring morning when the edges of new leaves curled like a paper telescope. I asked Grandma a

---

[6] Willa Cather, *Not Under Forty* (New York: Knopf Doubleday Publishing, 1936) 136.

question, then another. But she didn't answer, and looked at me as if she didn't know who I was. I felt a tearing in my middle, a feeling of inconsolable loss. And I *was* experiencing loss, for although I didn't know it then, that beautiful spring morning marked the onset of my grandmother's Alzheimer's. From then on, my image of her started to fade as if I were seeing her through a blurry lens. She seemed a stranger, not the grandmother who loved me, who picked and preserved cherries with me, the woman with whom I'd had a special bond; and I began making excuses why I couldn't visit.

For many years, I'd wanted to write about that day with my grandmother, knowing that while it might be painful, it would also be cathartic; and when enough time had gone by and I felt able, I found that it was. Writing the story enabled me to open to a new perspective and see the experience more clearly. I recognized my love for my grandmother, the special place she had in my life, and I also recognized my unwillingness to accept that she was disappearing before my eyes. Reflecting on what I'd written, a shudder of understanding washed over me.

None of us can get to middle age without regrets. The journeys over a lifetime and the evolution of my writing have brought me to where I am now. Age has had a way of softening how I take in blows, and even though I still feel the pain of loss, the passage of time has allowed me to accept it. Writing the story of Grandma helped, and luckily, it spurred another image of her—my grandmother in all her beauty gazing out the window. She turned and shined the beam of her smile towards me, warming the still-cold early morning kitchen. I felt peace, a sense of healing.

Living With Metaphor

Metaphors have a way of holding the most truth in the least space.

—Orson Scott Card, *Alvin Journeyman*

One of my favorite Ted Kooser poems is "Laundry," a short poem of only twelve lines, but as is Kooser's forté, it is packed with meaning. In the poem, a scene is painted for us. There is a pink house trailer and a clothesline on which the laundry hangs: "five pale blue workshirts / up to their elbows / in raspberry canes," and not far away, "a pair of bright yellow panties / urging them on." Wow! What does this have to say about the relationship of men to women, of ambition to love, about some of the basic driving forces of the universe?

It says a great deal, of course, and it does so in few words. Metaphors have a way of capturing the truth—what we feel we've known our whole lives but couldn't put into words—and in a flash, revealing it. As David Goleman explains, metaphors take "elements that symbolize a reality" and "speak directly to the emotional mind."[7]

I would go on to suggest that not only does metaphor have a way of revealing truths, of going directly to our "emotional minds," and making writing more powerful, but that *living with metaphor* will have the same effect. We recognize truths when they appear before us, and as a result, our days are richer and more meaningful. You look out your window and see cardinals flying across the backyard. Maybe they are hanging red streamers from tree to tree. You sit at your computer, pecking away at the keyboard and notice sparrows at the feeder pecking away too. Oh, those little bits of goodness you

[7] David Goleman, *Emotional Intelligence: Why It Can Matter More Than IQ* (London: Bloomsbury Publishing, 1995) 294.

all are finding! The just-right word that brings a smile to the lips; the sparrow's millet seed, delicious!

In a talk at the Iowa Summer Writer's Festival, poet Michael Dennis Browne encouraged his student poets to make a practice of memorizing poetry. Not only does it help to have poetic models in your mind, but (as Browne explained) if you're stuck in an elevator, you have a poem to keep you company. If you are feeling trapped, caged-in, you have images and playful thought to take you beyond the barriers that try to contain you; and on sleepless nights, you have poetry to occupy you until slumber finds you again.

You can do the same thing playing around with metaphors. They can entertain, and help you through difficult times. Let's say you wake in the middle of the night worried—about bills, about whether you said the wrong thing, about all the myriad sorts of things we humans find to worry about. Maybe we could turn worry into a metaphor. If worry were an animal, what would it be? Perhaps a mouse scuttling around in the walls. And what is this, really? Just a shy, scared little creature, a scuffling little noise, scurry, and a string of tail. It is nothing.

Or consider hope as metaphor. Sometimes hope is just a tiny flame, but you have newspapers shouting out bad news. You can shred them and add to the fire. You have old envelopes and rejection letters—add them, too! There are logs behind your house, you have an axe and it is sharp, and with these you can turn that little flame into a conflagration.

The mouse, the little fire, the newspapers and rejection letters— these are some of the "elements that symbolize reality." They speak to our emotional minds, help us see the truth and recognize the beauty around us. They help us get through the hard times to the other side.

Mysterious Healing Powers

The heart of man is very much like the sea, it has its storms, it has its tides and in its depth it has its pearls, too.

—Vincent van Gogh,
The Letters of Vincent van Gogh

We all need human companionship and a sense of connection and self-worth, whether we are living in the embrace of a nuclear family, as a widower in a subsidized apartment, or confined behind prison walls. The practice of art can be life-changing, its healing powers working in unfathomable ways to offer solace for loneliness and separation, and a renewed sense of purpose.

In a minimum-security prison in Maryland, inmates gather weekly in a cinder block room of the prison in order to knit. The men are of all ages, black and white, many big and burly and heavily tattooed. They are troubled men, men who have committed crimes, and they sit quietly at the tables, bending over their needles. One of their projects is to make comfort dolls, flat rectangles with faces, for children in domestic violence situations, children who have been removed from their homes often without even a blanket or book of their own.

As the weeks of knitting progressed, the inmates shared that *they themselves* were those children taken from their homes. "And [for] many of them," Lynn Zwerling, cofounder of the project, said, "the first hat they make, they make for themselves, or for children of theirs, children they haven't seen in maybe 17 years, children that they realize they're missing, they're lacking."[8]

---

[8] Lynn Zwerling, "Knitting Behind Bars, Learning Focus And Patience," interview by Michel Martin, *Tell Me More*, NPR News, January 9, 2012.

The Fire Inside

For a year, I taught writing to women inmates at a reformatory and saw how the women held each other accountable to a certain set of expectations, as if they belonged to a secret club with a code of unspoken rules. Male prisoners also have unwritten expectations of one another, and needlework is not generally considered an accepted activity for men to do. Yet the inmates of the Maryland prison project put aside any worry of possible exclusion in order to meet weekly and create dolls and hats from yarn.

Why did they do so? Initially, it might have been to satisfy a yearning for companionship in a comfortable situation. The knitting room was air-conditioned, and the women who conducted the class were enjoyable to talk with. But as time went on, it may have been that the desire to create took hold, and along with that, the realization that the clicking of knitting needles led them to discover gentler aspects of themselves, parts of themselves *they liked*. Perhaps the making, the creating of something with value, with purpose, touched them in profound ways, arousing in them a new consciousness about relationship and giving.

When we dedicate ourselves to our art, our sense of self expands and extends, and the lines between "we" and "they" disappear. The making of art gives life to something that didn't exist before. But they were only hats, some might say, only dolls. Still, we must allow for the mystery of creating, the tremble of art and of making, and of how the heart speaks through the workings of our hands.

Close to the Soul

Do you not see how necessary a world of pains and troubles is to school an intelligence and make a soul?

—John Keats, *Letters of John Keats*

There's a story about an enterprising French manufacturer who, after World War II, collected the brass from shell casings fired by German artillery to reuse in making musical instruments. The story goes that when melted down and recast, they made saxophones of world-class quality, some of the best saxophones ever made. And when the supply of German shell casings ran out and the manufacturer went back to pre-war materials, the newly manufactured instruments were somehow disappointing, unable to produce musical tones with the same resonance as before, the same richness.

There is some question as to whether or not this is a true story, but I like to believe that it is. I like to believe that the implements of war were transformed into the means for expressing great beauty, and out of all the horror came some sort of redemption. By no means making up for the tragedy of World War II, but *something*.

For isn't that what we do with our art? Take the raw material of our lives and turn it into poems or paintings or plays? Sometimes we create explosions of great jubilation, and at other times beautiful, meaningful work, but imbued with tinges of anxiety or despair.

As a young woman, Mexican artist Frida Kahlo suffered a horrific trolley accident in which she fractured her spinal column, along with her pelvis, ribs, collarbone, and foot. An iron bar pierced her abdomen, and her right leg was broken in eleven places. Doctors despaired of saving her, but she endured, suffering physical and emotional pain most of us cannot imagine. We see that suffering in her work, the violent and severe images, many of the paintings depicting not only her wounds from the accident, but others unseen to the eye and lasting her entire life. The paintings are troubling, but they are beautiful and true.

When my father died, I wrote out my heartbreak in poetry. When my mother became seriously ill, I did what I needed to care for her. I grieved, and kept on writing. As I look at those poems now, I consider them some of my best work, work of the soul.

When you write, Anne Sexton said, you should "put your ear down close to the soul and listen hard."[9] When we listen carefully, we know of pain. Life is beautiful and painful and joyous and fleeting. We grieve, we hurt. The other side of love is loss, and what can we do but live out our love, live through the loss; and if we are artists, create something beautiful from the broken shards, the vestiges of what has been lost.

---

[9] Anne Sexton, *No Evil Star: Selected Essays, Interviews, and Prose*, ed. Steven E. Colburn (Ann Arbor: University of Michigan Press), 2985.

Find Your Way

Artist was my identity.
—Karen Kunc, *in Hixson-Lied College Magazine*

Have you ever gone home for the holidays and heard—again—from beloved family members how accident-prone you are? (Remember the ditch? The neighbor's mailbox?) Or, perhaps, at a high school reunion your classmates still remember you as a *scaredy* cat? A nerd? The awkward girl hugging the wall at school dances?

A college student, Jeremiah, grew up in a family of clay potters but didn't seem to have the knack for working with clay; he didn't have the feel for it, the drive. His love was in drawing, especially drawing horses. In his childhood, he sketched and doodled and loved every moment. Then his fifth-grade teacher told him he didn't have talent, and he put his drawing tools away. In college, he became a business major but struggled, not really liking his classes, failing to see himself involved with administration of any sort, payrolls and endless columns of numbers.

Our early experiences shape us, help to form our identities, our perceptions of what we can and cannot do; and throughout our lives, we are continually cast back into situations akin to the childhood interactions that formed us. It's like being in a movie reel that keeps playing out the same dynamics again and again. As children we experienced fear, attachment, anger, sadness, and joy; we tried out athletics, music, and took part in the agony and ecstasy of school. In some instances we were praised, far too often we were found wanting, and so we built a sense of self.

As a child, how did you characterize yourself? Were you creative or predictable in your behavior? Were you one who came up with

41

a new idea, dove in, waited for others, took a risk, didn't change, listened carefully, or found a compromise? Today, how do you perceive yourself, and how do you act in response to these perceptions? Do you ask for a raise when you know you deserve one? Are you willing to try something again when you weren't good at it before?

From our earliest experiences and on through the course of our lives, personal identity is molded and continues to be refined by the bumping of relationships one against the other, the people we connect with having the potential to shape our lives. Their impact is powerful. Your sisters call you the "quiet one," and you retreat further and further into yourself. You're not that good at the game of catch, and when your father loses patience, when you're chosen last in various childhood games, you give up on any sort of athletics. You may identify yourself as too slow, too soft, too timid, one who lacks school smarts, street smarts, musical or other forms of talent. How can you ever get out of these ruts of negativity? How can you find your way?

Consider the character of Linus in the *Peanuts* comic strip. He's the younger brother of Lucy van Pelt, the best friend of Charlie Brown, but is defined primarily as the little kid who couldn't bear to be separated from his blanket. Then in kindergarten, when his teacher (who he adored) suggested he leave it at home, he did, finding it within himself to change. We, too, can change. But first, we must know in our bones that we have hidden potential, that we have the ability to grow into our more talented, absolutely amazing selves.

Late in his college career, Jeremiah transferred from the business to the art department, taking on the lifesaving task of developing his new identity. He was the wolf who avoided the trap, he said, the trap that kept him where he didn't want to be. Now he roams the hills with his drawing pad and pencils, sketching landscapes, pheasants in flight, and the horses he's loved since childhood, living into the self he's always wanted to be.

Opening Your Heart

To practice any art, no matter how well or badly, is a
way to make your soul grow.
　　　　—Kurt Vonnegut, *A Man Without a Country*

When we nurture our children, not only do we protect them, nourish their bodies and foster their intellect, we guide them into becoming the best version of themselves they can be. We nurture our art in the same way, and in the process, a funny thing happens. As we work to deepen our lives of the imagination, our creativity, in turn, works to nurture us, to encourage us to become more and better.

We make art out of an excess of passion and enthusiasm for a certain subject, creating art to share what we have found beautiful or wonderful or moving in some way, something which has affected us and which we want to share. We show our souls when we write, and we grow our souls. With every mosaic we create, every script we write, every emotion we are able to convey in a drawing or painting, we stretch a little—we grow, we become bigger than we were before.

We grow in patience, for making art requires patience. We grow in faith that things will work out, that effort will show a return, though perhaps not in the manner we intend when we begin. We develop the ability to see possibility in everything—the beauty of apples on a table or the way the light appears streaming through a stained-glass chandelier. We see the possibilities in others.

And we develop empathy. To become the best actors, writers, or artists we can be, we must inhabit the being of another. And so we learn compassion and appreciation for others—what it's like to live poor and on the margins in a culture infatuated with material wealth, to be overweight in a world (as my poet friend says) "too skinny to live." What it's like to experience shame. Of course we read and watch movies and take in visual art as consumers and experience empathy in that way, but we would contend that becoming for a while that other person—as we do in writing or acting—heightens the effect. Art is about paying attention to details, to seeing how the small seemingly insignificant detail is so profoundly important. How a supposedly "minor" character can make all the difference. Maybe we feel a little deeper, love a little greater.

"Art is a wonderful blessing if you use it," Brenda Ueland writes. "You will become happier, more enlightened, alive, impassioned, lighthearted, and generous to everybody else."[10] And you will open up your heart.

---

[10] Brenda Ueland, *If You Want to Write: A Book about Art, Independence and Spirit*, (BN Press, 2010).

For Your Journey

Speaking your joy or your pain through your stories and art can provide distance and give you a sense of freedom. What are you choosing to look at? Joanna Macy said that regardless of what we are facing, focusing on what we "truly, deeply long for" brings forth surprising results. Consider "where life is reinventing, encouraging us to find ever new ways," Macy added.[11] How do art and stories encourage and nurture you?

1. What family stories do you want to write and share? *Create a personal timeline starting at a young age to present day. Identify the major milestones of events or experiences, family rituals, celebrations, and the pictures that accompany them. Make a list of the experiences that arise for you. Select one or two where you observe a scene or a moment in rich details. Begin writing reliving those experiences.*

2. We all have secrets. Releasing them from their hiding places can bring light. Sometimes, transforming secrets through diverse art forms may shift the potency of the story or empower you to reinvent your own ending. *Consider choosing watercolor and photography—or whatever media you enjoy—and enter the secret gradually, without fear, and create, expressing your point of view.*

3. Mary Oliver asked: ". . . What is it you plan to do with your one wild and precious life?"[12] *Consider this question from three*

---

[11] Joanna Macy, Molly Young Brown. *Coming Back to Life: Practices to Reconnect Our Lives, Our World.* (Gabriola: New Society Publishers, 1998).

[12] Mary Oliver, "The Summer Day," *New and Selected Poems* (Boston: Beacon Press 1992).

perspectives: past, present, and future. If you were asked this question today, how would you answer? How did you answer fifteen years ago? What will you be able to say fifteen years from now? Share your insights with a good friend or create a poster that reminds you of what you plan on accomplishing in the future. Examples might include: make time for a friend, finish your degree, live by the mountains. You might want to photograph yourself smiling and add it to your poster. Display in a prominent place.

4. How do you manage your attention? What you choose to look at? *For thirty days, record what is summoning you, what gives you promise. When the month is over, where did you put your attention? What were the top three things that occupied your mind? Then ask yourself what's possible. What am I going to choose to put in my field of vision? Affirm your focus and make a creative portfolio of yourself. Name or draw all the ways you are creative.*

Chapter Three:
Choose to Live a Bigger Life

Big Dreams and Little Dreams

The answer is dreams. Dreaming on and on.
—Haruki Murakami, *Sputnik Sweetheart*

We all have dreams, though we are often fearful about voicing them, fearful even to spend time thinking about them. If we dare to dream, it's all the more hurtful if what we wish for doesn't come to pass; and perhaps, deep down, we may think we are too old, too ordinary. Who are we to dream such glorious dreams? But let's not think that way. The universe wants wonderful things for us.

What are your creative dreams? Do you want to write a mystery novel? Become proficient at dance? Maybe you want to paint a series of landscapes in each of the national parks. Dreaming is part of what it means to be human. To aspire, to have hope gives us purpose and makes us come alive; and to be truly, exquisitely alive, we must want something so badly we can taste it. Then be true to our desires and work towards coming as close as we can to realizing them.

The thing about big, wonderful dreams is that they do not easily come into being. Nothing worthwhile comes easy, the old saying goes; and since it can be a long, hard road working and waiting for what we yearn for to be realized, consider the idea of working toward *lots* of dreams—big dreams and little dreams, middle-sized ones too. Along with our big dreams of writing an award-winning mystery or hanging our paintings in the Museum of Modern Art, we can work on other goals at the same time. Submit an article to a magazine or create hand-made notecards. If you find that fulfilling, try collage or textile art. Why not? Are you a science fiction writer who delights in the joys of home winemaking? Consider writing an article—or even a book—about that. Don't count anything out. Let your mind open to the possibilities around you and see what happens.

The creative life is full of ups and downs. Reaching the pinnacle in a particular field is never guaranteed. If we could, I imagine we'd all like to be award-winning playwrights or artists, whatever the epitome of our particular passion might be; but it is not that which keeps us going. It is, instead, the relentless desire to "do art," as my friend Pam suggests, and "to feel how we feel when we're doing it." That's it. That's what's important . . . *that feeling*.

I believe dreams come true, but I also believe they can come true in ways we do not imagine. My husband, Tom, loved bluegrass music, and wanted to learn to play the banjo. But while waiting for repairs on the broken-down instrument he inherited, he started taking guitar lessons. After a stint with the guitar, he turned to the banjo, then cross-trained on the mandolin. Now the mandolin is his go-to, his instrument of choice. So it can be with other forms of the creative life. We may start out writing poetry and then develop an interest in fiction or non-fiction. Our growing expertise in one area leads to advancement in another.

Again, let's ask the question—what are your dreams and goals? Why not widen them, expand them, let the universe work its magic with the seeds of hope within? Dream big. But dream pint-sized and medium-sized too. Those little goals have a way of growing and developing in ways that can enrich your life immeasurably.

You Must Change Your Life

Keep on desiring. Keep on seeking.

—Lailah Gifty Akita,
Think Great: Be Great

Maybe you know the astonishing Rilke quote, "You must change your life," which is the concluding line of a poem written after reflecting upon a Greek sculpture of Apollo. The sculpture was created thousands of years ago and was severely damaged—by vandals, an earthquake, perhaps, or the relentless effects of time. Whatever caused the damage, the sculpture is armless and headless, but, Rilke asserts, *despite having no head*, "with eyes like ripening fruit," the torso, "still suffused with brilliance." It is as if there is great and vibrant power in the sculpture which is, after all, the *replication* of a *mythical god*, that replication created in stone, then partially destroyed. So the torso is several times removed from reality, and it is ruined. Still, Rilke sees the stone "from all the borders of itself/burst[ing] like a star."[13]

Then, of course, the dramatic ending, "You must change your life." It almost takes your breath away. The poem, I believe, speaks to the powerful and enduring nature of art; and in the remarkable last line, it is also speaking directly to us. Compelling us, commanding us, to change—to become all that we are.

There are within each of us great reserves of immeasurable potential, bestowed upon us at birth by a higher power. We were created of greatness, with greatness all around us, and we are capable of greatness we cannot imagine. We are part of the power of the universe,

---

[13] Rainer Maria Rilke, "Archaic Torso of Apollo," *Ahead of All Parting: Selected Poetry and Prose of Rainer Maria Rilke*, translated by Stephen Mitchell (New York: Random House Publishing, 1995).

ascendant and without bounds. So, let us accept it as a given that we have tremendous stores of creativity waiting to find form. Perhaps we don't know what our particular gifts might be. Or perhaps we don't have the confidence to acknowledge our talents, and use them.

Inwardly, though, a little voice may whisper: *Why not learn to play the violin? Why not try writing a poem, or taking a class in modern dance?* And indeed, why not? When we start listening to that little voice, we grow closer to what we are capable of.

Change can come in great dramatic cataclysms. We can quit our jobs, move to the coast of Maine, and begin to paint. Or it can come gradually—deciding to take an art class, trying to paint a little every day. Personally, we believe in slow but steady progress, knowing that each day will bring us closer to where we want to be.

How Music Elevates Us

To me, music is completely spiritual, it's the way you connect with your higher self, with the universe.

—Cindy Blackman,
Cindy Blackman Santana website

The morning traffic was terrible: congestion on Lookout Road, the streets an icy glaze, and I drove with my hands clutching the wheel, the muscles in my shoulders tightening into knots. At last I reached my destination, walked into my daughter's home and heard the beautiful strains of Bach's Minuet 5. My granddaughter was practicing the piano. Almost immediately, I was transformed, the frustrations en route behind me, my attention shifting to this new world of sound and vibration.

Nietzsche said that the primary task of music is "to lead our thoughts to higher things, to elevate, even to make us tremble . . ."[14] That cold February morning, Bach did just that, inviting me deeper into the melody, deeper into the innermost regions of the heart. The music spoke to me personally, collapsing time and taking me back sixty years to when I'd first learned and loved the minuet. And it spoke universally, connecting me to the many others who'd heard Bach's work, and like me, experienced transcendence. That day my world became a little bigger and a little more beautiful. Music, like all great art, speaks its own language and tells its own story. It also provides a universal form of communication, connecting us with others across time and space, uniting us in our common humanity.

And it does something more. It lifts us, speaks to our better

---

[14] Julian Young, *Friedrich Nietzsche: A Philosophical Biography*, (Cambridge University Press, 2010) 37.

angels, the part of us closest to the Divine; it inspirits us and makes us hopeful. It is so easy to fall into despair and cynicism, so easy to drown ourselves in the bad news of the world, and we must take care with the energies which surround us. Ensure that as much as possible we are immersed in that which uplifts, speaks to the nobility that is within, and to the good of the world. Wordsworth said that we come onto the earth "trailing clouds of glory."[15] Art reminds us of this, and that there is something bigger than we are, something sacred. Most of us cannot easily define this "something bigger" except to say that we feel it when we involve ourselves with art, when we take in goodness and beauty and contribute to its continued existence in the world.

I see this watching my brother-in-law, Brian, at the piano. He approaches the keyboard with great passion—focused, reverent, completely immersed in the handwriting of the piece, his muscles loose and free, his animal fingers taking on lives of their own, racing up and down the keys. He plays with his whole body, but he seems to play, also, *out of* the body. His brown eyes widen, then narrow to slits, his head swaying to some eternal rhythm. It is as if he is moved by a deep sense of yearning, as if he is connecting to some great and good immutable power. It is a feeling so strong, so visceral and yet so spiritual that he makes music with all that he is.

There are times we are closer to the Divine, when we remember that we came from magnificence and are part of the splendor around us. Great art in all its manifestations brings us closer to that magnificence and splendor. It elevates us, and as Nietzsche said, sometimes it makes us tremble.

---

[15] William Wordsworth. "Ode: Intimations of Immortality from Recollections of Early Childhood," *Poems, in Two Volumes*, (London: Longman, Hurst, Rees, and Orms, 1807).

Luminescent Individuality

*Life would be dull without experimenters and coura-
geous breakers-with-tradition.*

—Marie Bullock, *Letter to Stanton Coblentz*

You know those certain unique folks in your life—who live on the wild side? People with an unconventional bent who aren't afraid to dress in red to a black and white dinner party, skydive on their fortieth birthday, or who enjoy adding their novel, sometimes earth-shifting, viewpoints to a discussion? They are rare birds, the non-conformists, living out ways of being which are distinctly their own. In a world that does whatever it can to make you toe the line, what they do is remarkable.

Most of us live predictable lives, valuing and believing what our friends do, in sync with the majority. It's easy, and feels comfortable and secure, serene even. Yet the thrill of life, the spark, the joy comes not from security but the adventure of every day, the surprise around the corner. It comes from the new idea you try, because why not? And with that new idea, your life is opened up. When we surround ourselves with creative-thinking people, including non-conformists who will sometimes blow our minds, we're reminded of the delight that comes from listening to our own interior voices. We may find ourselves venturing from our customary patterns more often, taking more risks.

The most important awareness we have as living spirits is to be true to ourselves, and that means breaking out of cages that limit us. "True to your own solitude, true to your own secret knowledge," as poet Seamus Heaney suggests.[16] For artists, this is essential. We must live out our uniqueness, our special brand of creativity, to find our own secret knowledge. How can we do this? How can we live as luminescent individuals, the light of who we are shining from every cell? Living our individuality begins when we ask ourselves: *What do I really want? Believe?*

We can also ask, *Are my friends all alike?* Spending time with those who are different from us, we're able to depart from our normal ways of thinking. Consider art instructor Steve Snell, who took students pushing a covered wagon fifty-six miles on a portion of the Oregon Trail. It was winter, the temperatures hovering at twenty degrees, but they kept on; and along the way, collected "artifacts" to use in future paintings. Think how their experiences informed these students. How the challenging conditions and demands of a newly-created community influenced their artwork.

Living the life of the free spirit can mean writing about your torn fingernail, potatoes, the color green, or your daughter's first tooth—whatever idiosyncratic, off-the-wall, quirky thing that comes to mind. Or it can take the form of what may be perceived as a transgression, a violation of family "sanctity" by writing about abuse, alcoholism, the family story that-must-not-be-revealed. It can mean painting disturbing images of violence and dysfunction, composing songs about subjects which are only whispered about. We may make others uncomfortable in what we create, and it is always a personal decision as to whether we share it or not; but—and we can't stress this strongly enough—it is vitally important that we create it.

Ultimately, living as the one-of-a-kind people we are is about believing in ourselves, and about self-respect. As artists, it leads to the kind of art that can make a difference in the world.

---

[16] Seamus Heaney, "University of North Carolina at Chapel Hill, 1996," in *Take This Advice: The Best Graduation Speeches Ever Given*, (New York: Simon & Schuster, 2005, 85).

Wild Passions

Nothing great in the World has been accomplished without passion.

—G.W.F. Hegel,
Lectures on the Philosophy of History

About twenty years ago, after moving into a new house and acquiring a yardful of plants and flowers, I suddenly became obsessed with all things relating to flowers and flower-gardening—perennials, in particular. I checked out books from the library—*Perennial All Stars* and *Perennial Combinations* (two I remember), and pored through the pages. I loved everything about those books: the pictures, the descriptions of the various plants, and I especially loved their names—the elegant-sounding Lady's Mantle, exotic Siberian Iris and Golden Hakone Grass. There was Purple Toadflax—what *was* that? Silver Wormwood and Bear's Breech? It was as if there were years and years of mystery and ancient lore surrounding each herb and perennial, and I wanted to take it all in. I indulged myself in those books, and then in acquiring as many plants as would thrive in the twenty-by-forty patch of soil under my care.

When these wild passions make their appearances in our lives, each day is a little more exciting, each new encounter adding wonder and meaning and fulfillment. If we are lucky, we experience romantic passions. And meaningful relationships with family and friends. But if we are luckier still, we will experience all sorts of grand passions. Like passions for blues and reggae music, Asian food, and birdwatching. The more infatuations we have, the better. That's how we were meant to live in the world—like children finding delight in each new thing, like lovers wild for what we love.

From time to time, I've had flings with crewel embroidery, ceramics, and macramé. Those passions came and went. Others have been more enduring. I love the work of the poet, Mary Oliver, and have bought every book of hers I could lay my hands on. The same with Linda Pastan, Kim Addonizio, Dorrianne Laux, and Joyce Sutphen. A new discovery for me is poet George Bilgere, and I greatly admire the novelists Anita Shreve and Robert Morgan, Cormac McCarthy and Chris Bohjalian. There are many more, of course, and others I haven't discovered yet. The thought of that sends chills down my spine.

And now we come to that other great love affair we may experience—that with creativity, in whatever form it takes. "Passion is energy," Oprah Winfrey said. "Feel the power that comes from focusing on what excites you."[17] Let that passion burn. Embrace it. Take it to a beautiful place and make it yours forever. It's a wonderful way to be alive.

---

[17] Oprah Winfrey, qtd. by Caroline Castrillon in "5 Steps To Turn Passion Into Profit," *Forbes*, March 8, 2020, https://www.forbes.com/sites/carolinecastrillon /2020/03/08/5-steps-to-turn-passion-into-profit/#29e9cc3c700b.

Awaken to New Worlds

Literature . . . has shaped the lives of most humans on planet earth."

—Martin Puchner, *The Written World*

When my friends and I were starting high school, there was something special about the open arms of a shimmering summer. It wrapped itself around our hearts, lifted us up so that we fairly levitated in the radiance. Worries and frustrations seemed to evaporate, and we lived in an unintelligible sweetness like a summer romance. As we basked in its joys, however, we were aware of unknowns ahead, conflicts and personal questions difficult to resolve; and inwardly, we yearned for wisdom, insight, something to show us the way. Many of us turned to reading for answers, a particular book becoming a touchstone, its life-changing message offered like a personal Magna Carta granting us entrance to a new and awesome personhood.

We consumed books, mining literature for its gold not only for pure enjoyment and the opportunity to disappear into another world for a while, but to help us understand ourselves—and discover new ways of looking at the world. Reading opened us to new truths, and spoke to our interior lives. My quest, in particular, was in finding concrete explanations to questions I had regarding my personal values, especially as they related to the mores of the church and my community. *What did I believe in, really? And how could I reconcile those beliefs to the realities around me?* Before summer break that year, my English teacher, sensing my search for answers, suggested I read *The Nun's Story* by Kathryn Hulme. The plot centers on Sister Luke as she struggles with obedience and with conflicts in the decisions she faced. Each sentence, each paragraph seemed to speak directly to me, and when the last page came, I cast aside the beliefs and conventions that didn't fit anymore and claimed my own.

We think we are all alone with our problems, our heartache, and our despair—until we read. During college, Pulitzer prize winning writer Junot Diaz worked at a steel mill wearing thermal greens and metatarsal boots, toiling away at a job he hated. And when he wasn't working, consumed Toni Morrison's novels, reading with such deep concentration, that after lunch break, he could barely tear himself away from his book to go back to work. Her novels took hold of him, he said, as books do at "a certain age," and ultimately motivated him to become a writer.

Similarly, Cheryl Strayed, whose memoir, *Wild,* was made into a movie of the same name, found that reading opened up her life. At fifteen, she worked two full-time jobs, and in the spare minute or two she could find, dove into Dalton Trumbo's *Johnny Got His Gun*, and ate the book up. The book put her in a sort of trance, she said, "only of the reverse sort—not the kind that puts you under, but rather the kind that wakes you up."[18]

That's what we want and need, isn't it? To awaken to new worlds? For many of us, books are family, our lifeblood, offering us nourishment as essential as food and water. Books delight and inspire, they expand and shape our lives. They make us more than we would be without them. Vera Nazarian said: "Whenever you read a good book, somewhere in the world a door opens to allow in more light."[19] Oh, how we need that light, and how far we can go when it is shining down on the path before us.

---

[18] Cheryl Strayed, *Wild: From Lost to Found on the Pacific Crest Trail*, (New York: Alfred A. Knopf, 2012).

[19] Vera Nazarian, qtd. by Shahira Abdel Shahid in *Roadmap to Success: Inspiring Journeys of Ten Iconic Coptic Leaders*, (Bloomington: Archway Publishing, 2016).

Young at Heart

If I were to wish for anything, I should not wish for wealth and power, but for the passionate sense of potential, for the eye which, ever young and ardent, sees the possible.

—Søren Kierkegaard,
Either/Or: A Fragment of Life

Remember road trips? They were a great part of my childhood: summer, cruising along on back roads or two-lane highways, my sister and I throwing glances at one another, our hair flying, faces flushed. Row after row of DeKalb cornfields stretched endlessly, filling the mind with the unmistakable mathematical infinity where parallel lines never intersect, leaving no room for the cross purposes of worry or frustration. And with worries aside, the world grew in proportion, beautiful and endlessly fascinating.

What was at work? A youthful passion for exploration? Children's openness about the world? Young people have a way of seeing their surroundings through multi-colored glasses, perceiving novelty and perspective, surprise where more weathered minds see only the commonplace. Our greatest moments of creativity, we believe, come from an outpouring of beauty and powerful feelings. As a child, I saw that outpouring in the abundance in the fields and meadows. It was difficult to take it all in, mind-boggling, everything around me bubbling over with color and light.

As we know, a youthful outlook is not necessarily related to age. It is in seeing the world in both the small *and* the large, discovering the wonder in patterns as well as that which is seemingly without order. Recognizing abundance and possibility wherever we are. When we do this, even as adults with many years of the world pushing down on our shoulders, we start rethinking what holds meaning for us, what pulls us in, and we feel the world expand. We can retain this youthful state, no matter what our age.

It involves a mindset, a determination to take in wonderment whenever we encounter it: sitting on the porch or patio during a rainstorm and thrilling to the sudden chill, the grumble of thunder. It means catching yourself when you feel cynicism setting in. And it is in playfulness, seeing the world as a child. During the writing of *Moby Dick*, Melville said he rose every morning and gazed out his window as if it were the porthole of a ship, in a sense, "playing pretend." I see this same wide-eyed sensibility in my artist friends today. Julia writes a great deal of poetry on serious subjects, but breaks loose from time to time with a poem that is absolutely hilarious. Bonnie, a visual artist, feels the occasional need to paint a "joke" inside a painting, a barely perceptible animal or "funny face" peeking out of the intricate brushwork.

When we can keep alive the exuberance we had as children, our playful spirit, and the ability to be delighted again and again by birds and plants, the beauty of the plains and sky, we are among the luckiest people on earth.

The Poetry All Around

My inspiration comes from everywhere, everything, and everyone.

—Amelia Atwater Rhodes, *Falcondance*

I always thought the stork delivered me to the wrong home. Sure, I loved my family, the tidy little farm we lived on, but I realized early on that my life was on a different trajectory. My family was made up of hardy, pull-up-by-your-bootstraps kind of people, hard-working and principled. I admired them, but could not accept some of their precepts—for instance, that sick and dying animals were just part of farm life. I wore my heart on my sleeve, welling up at the barn cat who got his tail caught in the barbed wire fence, the baby calf abandoned by his mother. Crying at times when I was happy. I was emotional, my parents said.

Luckily, a smart teacher, sensing my tenderness, introduced me to poetry, including two poems that went on to become my favorites: Joyce Kilmer's "Trees" and "Wind on the Hill" by A.A. Milne. From these two, I went on to make poetry and the reading of poems a regular part of my life. Poetry connected me to a wider existence, helped me begin to comprehend that there are things in this world we cannot understand, that there existed something greater than I was. I began to realize that poetry could be found all around: in the daily actions of people, in the beauty of nature, everywhere.

Today, I still turn to poetry; it gives me pause and makes me wonder. I see its sweet language in the ordinary actions of people, in the way a mother feeds her toddler: the spoon as it rises—the hope and love that simple spoon ensures. I see it in the fervor of children at play, my three granddaughters engaging in the age-old game of Four

Square: the white ball's beat on the marked pavement, rhythmic and loud. Sometimes they sing a ditty, and when they're loose and wild and throw a low, fast dribble across the cement, they snort and laugh.

I remember my grandfather, after harvest, how he walked the empty cornfields gleaning, looking for one more ear of corn for the granary, for the cattle to make it through the winter. November and cold, but no matter how far he walked, he was always sure that *something good* was waiting for him. He had unshakeable faith. How can you make this world *yours*?

Poets like my grandfather, like mothers and children everywhere, reveal the intricate machinations of life, all beautifully connected, as indivisible from each other as the tides are from the ocean. Everywhere we look, we see clouds, sunlight, smiles, children, fields, families, and we see poems. There is poetry everywhere.

Dwell in Possibility

I dwell in Possibility –
A fairer House than Prose –
More numerous of Windows –
Superior – for Doors –

—Emily Dickinson, *The Poems of Emily Dickinson*

Vincent van Gogh is more than the creator of thousands of paintings, a guy with his ear cut off; he's a cultural icon, his life and art inspiring many of today's poems, books, film scripts, and music. Consider the lyrics to Don McLean's "Vincent." "Starry starry night," he wrote, "flaming flowers that brightly blaze."[20] Beautiful.

What is less well-known about Van Gogh is that he was also a prolific writer. In his surviving collection of letters, over 650 alone to his brother, Theo, we see the artist becoming more introspective as he matured. We also see—at a critical time in his life, failing in physical and mental health—how he used art as a means to slow down and begin a time of healing. Of his *Bedroom in Arles*, he wrote to his brother that he painted it "to be suggestive here *of rest* or *of sleep* . . ." that "looking at the painting should *rest* the mind, or rather, the imagination."[21]

In an elementary school in Lincoln, Nebraska, Visual Arts teacher Bob Reeker helped create a unique situation for students to experience art—by literally stepping into it. First, he transformed the school's media center into a three-dimensional, full-sized replica of Van Gogh's *Bedroom in Arles*—the wooden frame bed with its red blanket, the rattan-bottomed chairs, each and every detail of the painting. Then, he

---

[20] Don McLean, "Vincent," *American Pie*, United Artist Records, 1971.

[21] Vincent van Gogh, Letter to Theo van Gogh, 16 October 1888.

invited students to "go inside" the painting, to dwell there a while and take photographs of themselves. Finally, he asked them to write letters to Van Gogh's brother describing their snapshots. "What meaning did the experience have for you?" he asked the students, and they found themselves thinking in ways they hadn't thought before, wondering what it would be like to live long ago, what it would be like to meet Van Gogh. "I went crazy," one student enthused.

When we encounter art, possibilities open, and we feel a kinship with the work. But we must be alive and curious, ready to engage with the imagination, ready to enter into new realities where shades of light, images or objects in nature give rise to new form. And then the artwork comes to life in the viewer's mind in a way that transcends the frame which attempts to contain it.

In addition, questions arise: *What message is conveyed? How do the symbols inform us?* And most importantly, *how am I affected?* When we allow ourselves to fully engage with great art, we feel a responsiveness, a personal relationship, almost as if we are involved in an intense dialog with the work. Sometimes we may become a little unsettled, always we will be moved and changed.

When we take time to interact with art, we set our imaginations on fire. And when we do, a one-dimensional painting can become a new world. Providing, as Emily Dickinson so aptly described, an amazing opportunity to "dwell in Possibility."[22]

---

[22] Emily Dickinson, "I Dwell in Possibility (466)," *The Poems of Emily Dickinson, Reading Edition*, ed. Ralph W. Franklin (Cambridge: The Belknap Press of Harvard University Press, 1998).

Work and Meaning

The job is what you do when you are told what to do . . .
I call the process of doing your art 'the work.'

—Seth Godin, Linchpin: *Are You Indispensable?*

There is a difference between the jobs we do and our work. We *have* to do our jobs, whether we consistently find meaning in them or not; but our work is sustaining, it is holy. It compels us to get up in the morning itching to get to our paints, to the song we are composing. It gives purpose to our days.

"I don't have a job," writer Richard Russo said, "but I have tons and tons of work. The work sustains me. I'm doing something that gives my life meaning, it connects me to other people."[23] He went on to define his work as that of a writer, but also as husband and father of two daughters.

If we are fortunate, like Russo, our "work" coincides with what we do to fill the bank account. Meaning and the making of money go together. In too many cases, however, and especially for those who find their life's work in the arts, that doesn't happen. It's difficult to make a living as a poet or singer-songwriter, so we do what we must to keep a roof over our heads and provide for our families. We do our jobs and in them strive for meaning—in the relationships we make, the good we can do within the context of those jobs. At the same time, however, we make room in our lives for our "real" work, that which pulls at us and excites us. That which is a calling, similar to a spiritual calling. For me, this is writing. For our photographer friend, Charles,

---

[23] Richard Russo, interview by Renee Montagne, Author Richard Russo Ponders What The Presidential Election Was Really About, *Morning Edition*, NPR, November 10, 2016.

it means traveling the world in search of unforgettable images, then capturing them on film.

"This is satisfying work," my poet friend said of editing the poems in her latest manuscript, arranging the pieces into a whole, refining, working on the details. And when one book is done, one painting, one play scripted and performed, it is time to work on another. Find a contented person, and you will find one immersed in a project.

Work means making and polishing, striving for a certain look or feel, striving for a certain something that may be impossible to define. It also means changing as our lives do, and finding meaning in new ways. For Julia, writing poetry has always been a major part of her work. But as she grows in her craft, teaching and conducting workshops are taking on a great importance as well. In his later life, while continuing to create stunning images through his paintings, Monet also designed and brought forth beauty in his garden in Giverny. This was part of his work. And so we go about living our lives—doing our work as well as our jobs, finding meaning and purpose.

For Your Journey

In the Calvin and Hobbes cartoon series of the late eighties, six-year-old Calvin remarks to his stuffed tiger friend, Hobbes: "I say, if your knees aren't green by the end of the day, you ought to seriously reexamine your life."[24] I love that. The young child's recognition that we need to play hard, go hard, get down on our hands and knees and roll around in life. In other words, make our lives as "big" as we can. And, of course, I'm not talking about a big house or car or vacation or a big important job. But a life big in experience, a life rich in meaningful relationships and meaningful work.

1. An important part of one's life work is discovering, identifying just exactly what that work is. And in that work, of course, are many different areas of responsibility. You might identify your life's work as painting, being a wife and mother, or doing what you can to save the natural ecosystem in your state. *Take some quiet time and consider your life's work, and jot down at least three elements of what you see as your work, keeping in mind that this will change many times over your lifetime.*

2. In order to open to new experiences and widen your relationships, you may need to limit some activities. *Take out a sheet of paper and brainstorm the activities you do on a regular basis. Place a check mark before those activities you feel enhance and enrich your life, and cross out those you may want to draw back from. Find at least five of the latter, those things that do not add greatly to your life but you keep doing out of habit or a sense of duty. You might want to eliminate*

---

[24] Bill Waterson, *The Essential Calvin and Hobbes: A Calvin and Hobbes Treasury* (Kansas City: Andrews McMeel Publishing, 1988).

elaborate meal preparation, or drop out of organizations that don't seem to fit any longer. What would you name?

3. Think back to some of the passions you have had in the past— as a child or younger adult. Perhaps you were crazy about rock and roll or rock collecting. Maybe you had a stint with acting in high school and at one time felt this would be something you'd do more of. *Many of these "wild passions" of our younger days we let go by the wayside. Are there any you'd consider taking up again? Exactly as you did in the past or in a slightly different form? Take a moment and name two or three of these. More, if you can. What other fancies are in your mind, perhaps just below the surface of consciousness? Let these come out into the open.*

4. Visualize yourself a year from now living a bigger life. Where are you? What are you doing, and who are you with? *Now gather some crayons and markers and draw a picture of yourself living this exciting, enriched new life, doing what you want, living as you may not have imagined before. Take some time with your drawing, sketching in details of your surroundings, what you are wearing, and hints as to your activities. Have some fun with this.*

PART TWO:
INTO THE MYSTIC

The universe is full of magical things patiently waiting for our wits to grow sharper.

—Eden Phillpotts, *A Shadow Passes*

Chapter Four:
Look for the Mystery

When the Universe Calls

Everyone has a creative potential and from the moment you can address this creative potential, you can start changing the world.

—Paulo Coelho, *interview with Reuters*

Novelist and teacher Lee Martin wrote an article entitled "Saying Yes," about accepting a request to speak before a group of aspiring writers. He had much to do—preparing for classes, writing recommendations for his students, and spending time on his own writing. However, Lee said, he likes to say yes in these kinds of situations. So he spoke to the group—telling them about general writing practices, reading one of his essays, and conducting a question and answer session. After the Q & A, a writer came up to him and told him he'd given him food for thought about a story he was working on. "That's why I say yes," Lee wrote. "I know there's always a chance I'll say something that will make a difference for someone."[25]

And this is one of the best reasons, we believe, that when the universe comes to us with a story idea, a poem, or inspiration for a new art project, we must do all we can to say yes and answer the call. The poems and stories we write are gifts that are given to us. Some of them are just for us, to be kept for ourselves. (You know the ones.) But some are meant to be passed on, to be shared. When we write out of our

---

[25] Lee Martin, "Saying Yes," Lee Martin Author Page, September 22, 2014.

deepest emotions, expressing feelings of love, loss, disappointment, despair—all the passions involved in being human—we create the potential for connection. We never know when a particular piece we write will resonate with another, and provide a moment of inspiration or understanding. Maybe it will help someone through a tough time.

We might feel skeptical about some of the ideas the universe suggests, fearful they would be considered "navel-gazing," or self-indulgent. But we believe it is important to say *yes*, anyway; and fearlessly continue to say *yes* as we pay attention to where the universe and our hunches guide us. For we, too, are worthy of inspiration and of help during difficult times, and our art might be exactly what we ourselves need. If, at the same time, we can help someone else, then all the better.

There are times to say no—to work which does not come from our deepest selves, which does not feed our souls. And at times when we are overwhelmed. But there are times to say yes—to writing, and sharing what we have written—through publication, reading at an open mic, or sharing with a group of friends. "The purpose of life," Leo Rosten said, is to matter, to be productive, to be useful, to have it make some difference that you lived at all."[26] We can do this every day by saying yes when the universe calls out to us, offering ways to use the creative potential we've been given.

---

[26] Leo Rosten, "The Myths by Which We Live," *The Rotarian* 58, no. 3 (1965): 55.

Blue Horses

I step into the painting of the four blue horses / I am not even surprised that I can do this.

—Mary Oliver, "Franz Marc's Blue Horses"

One Christmas I received as a gift the Mary Oliver book, *Blue Horses*, and was blown away by it—first of all because I've admired Mary Oliver's writing for ages, and secondly, because of the book's *cover*. This features a painting of four horses, their forms rounded and graceful, all looking to the left as if something has caught their interest—a fox, a dog, or a person. The horses are beautiful and blue, the background in shades of yellow, spangled with stars, as are the horses themselves, their heads and bodies starry, so whether the horses are of the earth or the heavens, we are not sure.

The painting is by Franz Marc, an expressionist painter and member of the "Blue Riders," a group of artists in Germany in the early 1900s. Marc was talented and influential, but in 1916 during World War I, his career was cut short when flying shrapnel struck him in the temple and he was killed. He was just thirty-six years old.

I imagine Mary Oliver, as she describes in her poem, "stepping into" the painting, the horses coming to her and touching her with their noses. She thinks about the horses and the man who imagined and painted them, and who died too soon. "I would rather die than try to explain to the blue horses what war is," she wrote.[27]

This is a beautiful poem about a beautiful painting. More and more, I find myself intrigued by visual art, loving art for itself, and interested by what I see as the connection between painters and writers, both

---

[27] Mary Oliver, "Franz Marc's Blue Horses," in *Blue Horses*, (New York: Penguin Books, 2016).

groups working out of an image or thought or essence at the corners of their minds. That certain something which is elusive, but which we catch glimpses of from time to time—when our work goes well, when we're in the flow, or even, if we're lucky, when we're walking, mowing, or filling up the car. All of us, whether artists or writers, are seeking that essence, trying to capture it on paper or canvas before it flits away.

It has been suggested that writing poetry is an effort to express what ultimately cannot be put into words. Perhaps it's more than that. Poetry may serve to remind us of the truths we once knew. There are verities at the edge of consciousness, vitally important, but which often elude us. This is what we struggle with, and why we keep at it. We do our work. We grow closer, and once in a while, we succeed. And, as Mary Oliver said, "maybe the desire to make something beautiful / is the piece of God inside each of us."[28]

---

[28] Ibid.

A World with Infinite Connections

*There is no such thing as chance; and that which seems
to us blind accident stems from the deepest source of
all.*

—Friedrich von Schiller,
Sunbeams: A Book of Quotations

Every time it happens, I light up with joy. I find myself in unexpected places and with people I never planned on meeting, and discover in their associations hints that we live in a world where everything is beautifully connected. Taking a poetry class led to finding a writing group, and my experience there led to the publication of a book. Having my lease unexpectedly cancelled forced me to move to a new apartment where I met my life partner. Were these occurrences all part of my destiny, my fate? There is an astonishing sort of harmony in the world, an underlying pattern in seemingly unrelated events.

When we commit to living creatively, we see these patterns in our lives, and a spirit world of lines, shadows, and color reveals itself. To enter, we first must trust, then follow our passions and deepest instincts, no matter where they lead. Being open to the unknown requires both patience and awareness, and for many of us, a vulnerability that may be uncomfortable. But if we follow these whispers of instinct down new paths which test our skills and abilities, remarkable things can happen. "Hummingbird moments," my pastor calls them for the delight and surprises they bring.

Robert, a friend and master photographer, once told me how unplanned things in his life often seemed to converge, referring to them as "magic moments of synchronicity." In these moments, he said, he felt as if wonderful vibrations were running through his body, as if an enormous bell were being struck inside him. One day, walking and planning a photo shoot of a Nebraska sunset that was to take place the following evening, little things started catching his attention. He noticed how his neighbor's new pine tree gave depth to the front yard. Later, he stopped to watch mallards feeding and swimming in a lake. In the water, a glorious interplay of pale yellow and red lights danced before him, drawing his eyes, he believes, to what was important. The next day, when a perfect, flaming sunset surrounded the pine tree, he realized that this was what he had been waiting for. "Bingo!" he said and shot an unforgettable photo.

We, too, can find similar moments, connect the dots, and discover what is waiting for us and our creative lives. The world is infinite in its capacity to support us, but we must recognize for ourselves the spark of inspiration when it appears. It's about paying attention and listening to our instincts, whether they are felt as the vibrations of a giant bell or the faintest murmurings of an idea, and then following where they lead.

AWE-Some

Perhaps it is not so much what we learn that matters in these moments of awe and wonder, but what we feel in relationship to a world beyond ourselves, even beyond our own species.

—Terry Tempest Williams, *The Hour of Land, A Personal Topography of America's National Parks*

I am standing before the North Dome at Yosemite National Park for the first time, and become very still. The granite dome is an astonishing display of form and texture, the play of light and shadow making me feel I could stretch out my fingers and touch the diamond-patterned surface. It's like old lace frozen in time, or swirled chocolate and caramel fudge. I'm fascinated, mesmerized. What I am feeling is the overwhelming emotion of awe.

The view of such a beautiful scene in nature can be mindbending, turning our attention outwards instead of inwards. This, Nira Liberman finds, inspires the experience of awe. She describes an awe-filled moment as one provoking "expansive thought," a process in which looking at objects at a remove fosters flexible thinking and the development of different perspectives.[29] Much like flexing your muscles to weight train, when we experience awe we enhance the agility of our thought processes, often leading to greater openness and the discovery of more pathways to creativity.

It's good to remember, however, that expansive thought doesn't

[29] Nira Liberman, Polack, O., Hameiri, B., & Blumenfeld, "Priming of spatial distance enhances children's creative performance," *Journal of Experimental Child Psychology* 111, no. 4 (2012): 663-670.

require the sort of grand-scale experience that I had at Yosemite. We can feel a shift in perspective as we take in the shimmering red maple trees along a fence line or the tranquility of the neighbor's pond with its curtain of cattails. Or love. Remember that first intense love relationship? How you were overwhelmed with rapture, weak in the knees? Then there's the simple beauty of a moonless night, the stars as if they were cutouts in a swirl of purple cloth. Awe-filled moments like these make us feel more alive, more connected.

One evening, standing in the Atlantic Ocean, I ran my hand through the water and a ribbon of beautiful blue lights undulated before me. They were "fire plants," I later learned, tiny marine plankton emitting sparks and lighting up the ocean. The tide came in, and a circle of blue luminance rose above my ankles and shins, splashing up towards my knees. I was a little disoriented, dumbstruck. Then came the gravitational pull of the sun and the moon. I felt the water falling away, the blue lights falling away, pulling me back into the ocean's immensity. It was as if I were a small blip in this giant body of water, a minute cell in this whole wondrous universe.

Such illuminating, awe-filled moments are rare and fleeting, but their impact alters us. Listening to violinist Joshua Bell, we're enraptured, riding along with each resonant choice he makes, enthralled. Beholding Claude Monet's tranquil water lily painting, *Nymphéas*, we might be moved to aesthetic arrest, his art so beautiful we have no choice but to pause and try to take it in. Experiencing awe inspires us, shakes us loose, propels the creative passion inside to rise like sap in springtime. It is as if we are given a point of reference for what is possible, prompting us to reflect on the miracles that await.

Sweet Dirt

*I think poems return us to that place of mud and dirt
and earth, sun and rain.*

—Kevin Young, *The Hungry Ear*

On my knees, working in my flower garden, I put my ear to the earth and listen. Often, the earth talks back. Over there, she says, do a little spading before winter sets in so snowmelt can get to the roots. Add a little extra fertilizer here or spread some topsoil. Move this rosebush: too much shade, more sunshine, please.

John Keats wrote that "The poetry of the earth is never dead," and I believe that.[30] As a child, I loved to spend time on my grandparents' farm where everything vibrated with life—the trees, the grass, the solitary rocks, and especially the open fields of plowed ground. I loved the promise of spring; I loved the harvest. I spent hours exploring the silvery creek that zigzagged across one of the fields. If I sat quietly on its banks for a while, I might spot tiny faces poking up from the wet earth—little moles, noses wiggling as if trying to connect.

Tracy Kidder and Richard Todd in their book, *Good Prose*, suggest that when you write, you "place yourself on the page as in part self-discovery, in part self-creation."[31] They compare the practice to that of a sculptor working with marble—questing, searching, removing a bit of stone here, chipping away some there, always looking, knowing that somewhere in the stone there is a face, a form. Of course, there is mystery in bringing the sculpture to life, but certain elements stand

---

[30] John Keats, "The Grasshopper and the Cricket," in *Poems* (London: C. & J. Ollier, 1817).

[31] Tracy Kidder and Richard Todd, *Good Prose*. (New York: Random House 2013), 51.

out like the mountains and valleys on a relief map. These elevations become the true *face* of that person.

My mother's life was not about the great struggles and hardships she experienced, nor even the joys and contentment she knew with her family. Rather, it was about the unrealized relationship between herself and the earth. She survived the Depression but ended up moving around from farm to farm during her long life, connecting deeply to each plot of land, though never owning the land and hills she loved.

In African cosmology, there's a belief that spirits persist in the earth, conveying words of support and encouragement to those who work the soil. Assisting as the world keeps making itself, sharing its bounty. I have to wonder if Mother's great-great-grandparents, those who worked the land through many generations of hardship, knew this wisdom, and realized the earth's power.

Why think about all of this? Because there are things we haven't said out loud, perhaps haven't fully realized, and we have an opportunity to make a little more sense of the world. We are born of the earth, and like the sweet soil from which we are made, we long for ways to replicate ourselves, through our bodies, and also through the glorious creations of our hearts and minds.

Waiting for Grace to Fall Down on Me

*I do not at all understand the mystery of grace—only
that it meets us wherever we are but does not leave us
where it found us.*

—Anne Lamott,
Traveling Mercies: Some Thoughts on Faith

There is something seductive in a good short story—each scene nuanced and packed with meaning, a feeling that *each* image is important, *each s*crap of dialogue. And often, as in the work of Alice Munro, Canadian Nobel prize-winning author, there is a feeling that *I'm being let in on a little secret,* but that perhaps *I'm not quite catching it. Not all of it, anyway.*

In one of her stories, "Dance of the Happy Shades," the narrator is attending a piano recital put on by Miss Marsalles, spinster and piano teacher for years, now in reduced circumstances. Her parties are an embarrassment, with Miss Marsalle's fussiness and old-fashionedness, her students' limp performances. And this year things are even worse. Many of the invited guests do not appear, and there is concern about the party fare—sandwiches set out hours ago, the punch going flat. The pieces played are halting and uninspired.

The recital is nearly over when a new group arrives, special needs students who have not appeared at previous recitals. They are dressed shabbily, their faces docile and eyes slanted, and when they begin to play, they are no worse than anyone else and no better. That is, until one of the new students, a "plaintive-looking" little girl sits down to play. What emerges from beneath her fingers is "fragile," and "courtly," expressing "great unemotional happiness." The room grows quiet, the guests realizing they are hearing something extraordinary, music played with such natural feeling and elegance and joy that it is a gift. It is grace falling down for Miss Marsalles, for everyone who hears.[32]

Flannery O'Connor has written that "a story is good when you continue to see more and more in it, and when it continues to escape you."[33] That is how I feel about "Dance of the Happy Shades." A roomful of recital guests prepare to endure a tiresome party and grace falls down on them. O'Connor also writes that she is "interested in characters who are forced out to meet evil and grace," and the characters decide whether or not "to accept their moment of grace."[34]

Isn't this how we live our lives? Going out every day to see what we can see and meet what is put before us? Hopefully, when grace falls down on us, we will be awake enough and wise enough to accept it. And isn't this how writing works? Writing to figure things out, to look at mystery and make sense of our lives? We put down one word after another, and sometimes the words come to us as gifts.

I am still trying to learn how to write the kind of story that O'Connor talks about, one that upon reading and rereading reveals more and more, but ultimately remains elusive. I am waiting for that grace to fall down on me.

---

[32] Alice Munro, "Dance of the Happy Shades" in *Dance of the Happy Shades* (Whitby, Ontario: Ryerson Press, 1968).

[33] Flannery O'Connor, "Writing Short Stories" in *Mystery and Manners: Occasional Prose* (New York: Farrar, Straus and Giroux, 1970).

[34] Ibid.

I Didn't Know I Loved

So many believe that it is love that grows, but it is the knowing that grows and love simply expands to contain it.

—William P. Young, *The Shack*

In the fall of my sophomore year in college, I met an intriguing young man in my English class. He was red-haired, wore desert boots and an army jacket ("cool" attire of the times); he was funny and sweet, and there was that "something" about him. Three times he'd taken me out, but at the end of each evening, there was just a quick goodbye kiss at the dorm elevator. What was wrong? I was ready for two kisses in a row, at least. Maybe three.

One day after class, he said he'd gotten a new bluegrass album, and maybe I'd like to come to his apartment and listen to it. That is, *if* I liked bluegrass. I had a moment of panic—I had no idea what bluegrass music might be. But I decided to take destiny into my own hands. "I *love* bluegrass music," I said. And that evening, after listening to the record, two things happened. First of all, let me say, the heat index of our romance went up significantly, and secondly, I found that I *did* love the high and lonely sound of bluegrass.

This is the story of how my husband and I met, and I tell it now with the thought that maybe there are many things in the world we don't know we love. And it is not until we come face to face with them and give to them kind and thoughtful consideration that we realize the extent of our liking, our high regard, our absolute delight in what is before and around us.

Writing and creating art, I believe, helps us to discover what it is we love. On a train from Berlin to Prague, Turkish poet Nâzim Hikmet wrote, "I never knew I liked / night descending like a tired bird on a smoky wet plain." How beautiful, that tired bird. "I never knew I liked the night pitch-black," he continues, "sparks fly from the engine / I didn't know I loved sparks."[35] I imagine him on the train, pen to paper as night comes on, writing, and with each line discovering more and more of what he loved. For we *do* uncover new realities when we live creatively. How wonderful to find what we love, and how rich it can make our lives!

---

[35] Nâzim Hikmet, "Things I Didn't Know I Loved," in *Selected Poems of Nâzim Hikmet* (New York: Persea Books, 1975) 80.

Beneath the Prairie Sky

One fancies a heart like our own must be beating in every crystal and cell, and we feel like stopping to speak to the planets and animals as friendly fellow mountaineers.

—John Muir, *Nature Writings*

Visit Spring Creek Prairie near Denton, Nebraska, and you will see the dazzle in everything. It's like walking into a green-lit cathedral and discovering radiance for the first time. You look out over swaying grass, and a thousand shades of gold and green greet the eye. There's a richness of flora and fauna, a feeling of endless spaciousness, and above, a sky with no edges. Eastern phoebes and red-winged blackbirds dip and soar, and jackrabbits skedaddle from beneath bunchgrass and bull thistle. The prairie vibrates with light and life.

In *The Power of Myth,* Joseph Campbell wrote that many Native Americans addressed the rocks, the rivers—everything—as "thou." The earth and all its elements were considered sacred, precious, "the air [sharing] its spirit with all the life it supports," the "perfumed flowers . . . our sisters."[36] When we acknowledge that all things are connected, we can develop a sense of the sacredness existing around us. To accomplish this, however, some of our fixed ideas about the world will need to change.

Consider the Argiope, the yellow garden spider, who lives in the prairie and weaves her web between blades of Big Bluestem or Switchgrass. It's perfect there, for even in a gale the silk holds fast because of the give and take, the strands of web moving along with the grasses. If our spider had chosen to place her web between two

---

[36] Joseph Campbell, *The Power of Myth* (New York: Anchor Books, 1988).

hard objects like rocks, a strong wind would stretch and break the fine lines. How does she know this? The natural world is full of mystery, having more complexity and intelligence than we ever imagined.

Recently, walking into the prairie with new awareness, I let my eyes rest on my surroundings, and soon an object appeared—a small, reddish rock. Every other day, I'd have referred to the shard of granite as "it." That day, the name shifted to "thou." Farther along, a fallen branch crisscrossed the path in front of me. *Thou branch*, I thought. *When did you fall from your beloved tree?*

What if we live as if rock, branch, lizard, fern, and wind were all sentient beings with their own kinds of consciousness? Then, the beautiful offerings of nature would open the doorway to wonder and a sense of reverence. We'd feel a connectedness to all. If we could behold this world as *thou world*, what changes would we see? And what marvels would open up before our eyes?

In our lives and in our creative lives, we must be like the Argiope spider, at peace trusting our intuitive biology, and feeling the connectedness with the vibrant and spirited world around us. All the while listening to the wind, the whispers of stones, the quiet rustling of the grass.

What Are We "About"

To be a great artist, life is about searching for some-
thing that gives you an insatiable craving to go further
and beyond.

—Talismanist Giebra, *Talismanist: Fragments of*
Ancient Fire: Philosophy of Fragmentism

What is it we are "about" when we write? When we paint or produce a play? What are we *after?* Is it a certain feeling or mood, an emotional response? Maybe like the impressionist painters, it involves a specific goal, such as capturing the play of sunlight and shadow, accurately portraying the luminosity of light on water. Maybe, like Cezanne, the goal is to paint an apple that is both the essence of apple, and an apple with such form and solidity that you could almost extend your hand and pluck it from the canvas.

Attempting to put into words our goals and desires as artists is difficult. What are we endeavoring to bring to light one completed canvas after another, one design after another? What are we after? These are questions that go to the heart of who we are as writers and artists, our identities as individuals living in the world.

As a fiction writer, it is important to me to establish a strong sense of place, conveying the immensity of the plains under a blue bowl of sky, or the desolate beauty of the desert—and the emotional implications of each. There I place my characters and follow them as they live out their joys and heartaches against the backdrop of that landscape. I am also "after" a certain spareness in my writing, revealing powerful emotions in a restrained manner.

A poet friend says of her writing that she wants to discover that truth she did not realize she knew, the truth she learned in the womb before she was born. What we are about can be said to be composed of many elements, and will change and evolve as time goes on. Some days we may just want to "write a good story." Or paint a picture reminiscent of Renoir or Cassatt. Like restless children, we may not be able to put our fingers on exactly *what it is* we want. We can't say. But it is *something*—just out of reach, coming into our grasp from time to time and then gone. We may catch fleeting glimpses of that elusive something—in a paragraph we write, electric with meaning, or in the fervor in a face we sketch. And all our lives struggle to rediscover that electricity, that fervor.

"I'm just a pilgrim on this road," Steve Earle wrote.[37] And yes, we all are pilgrims, seeking out that intangible element, that certain component or spark that will set our hearts racing, make the hairs on the backs of our necks stand on end. And know we are on the right track.

---

[37] Steve Earle, "Pilgrim," recorded 1998, track 14 on *The Mountain* E-Squared, compact disc.

From the Body

Writing begins in the body, it is the music of the body, and even if the words have meaning, can sometimes have meaning, the music of the words is where the meanings begin . . . Writing as a lesser form of dance.

—Paul Auster, *Winter Journal*

We human beings have some spark in us, a spirit which makes us who we are. We have intelligence that allows us to reason, make connections, and create from what is around us. But we are also of the physical world, of the body. We are made of dust, it is said. We are housed in our bodies, stay alive through our bodies, and act out of them. We must listen from the body and feel from the body. Words come from our vocal cords, are manipulated with our tongues, and emerge from between our lips. When we write, the words come down through our arms to our fingers where we can set them down on the page in black and white.

We speak of writing *from the heart*. When we know the truth of something, we say we feel *it in the gut,* we know it *in our bones*. And when we read good writing, we are *touched*. A friend speaks to us to share his point of view. "I see," we respond. "I hear you." When we write, we must depend not only on our mental capacities, our abilities to reason. We must allow whatever wants to arise to flow out of our bodies.

One night, our writing group wrote about "our favorite body parts." We had a great time with that. One member wrote about how she liked her arms, how flexible they were and how she could fold her grandchildren within them. Another wrote of her hair, her crowning glory. Leo wrote a wonderful tongue-in-cheek piece about his big toe!

We did a lot of laughing that evening, but we also felt that we had written truths we don't usually acknowledge.

We stockpile hurt in our bodies, both physical and emotional, and when we create art, we go deep within to access that emotion. We store happiness too, our bodies almost singing in moments of bliss. Not only do we hunger physically, we hunger emotionally and spiritually as well, and in writing and sharing what we have written, we are nourished.

For Your Journey

How does it happen that the idea for your next project seems to drop suddenly in your lap? That you struggle for months over the ending for your novel, then decide to follow that troublesome thread tickling around in your mind, and *voila!* There it is. These are happenings we cannot explain, enigmas that give us pause. "The universe buries strange jewels deep within us all," Elizabeth Gilbert says, "and then stands back to see if we can find them."[38] The key to finding them, we believe, is through close attention. Call it listening to your gut, or call it the result of forces greater than we are, some "magic" seems to be in play. We can grasp onto that magic and have it take us along.

1. *For a month or more, keep a journal of the coincidences and synchronicities that come your way: the reading you almost didn't attend but where you meet the writing partner you have been longing for. The times you encounter multiple references to the same book, and when you decide at last to read it, your life is changed. Is the universe working to tell you something? To help you along? It may sound a little "out there," but when we keep our minds open, pay close attention, and act upon the signals we receive, amazing things can happen.*

2. As artists and human beings, we tend to focus on our problems, what we don't have: the kudos our friends receive and we do not, the literary agent we desperately want, that firm connection with a theater group. Negativity doesn't help, and it is said that when we give, we receive. Why not try the practice of gratitude? *Every evening before you go to sleep, express your*

---

[38] Elizabeth Gilbert, *Big Magic: Creative Life Beyond Fear* (New York: Riverhead Books, 2015), 8.

silent thanks to the powers that be for what you are grateful for that day. Thank you for my art room, you might say to the night, for my writing desk, for the color I found that is just right for my new painting. Thank you for the kind words my friend said. Speak into the dark and let your good thoughts, your gratitude, go up and out into the universe.

3. What is it that you didn't know you loved? *Take a walk in a public garden or along a forest trail. Put your senses on high alert. What colors do you see? What shapes? What sounds and aromas do you encounter? Now ask yourself, what do I see and smell and feel and hear that I love? Maybe you didn't know you loved the color yellow, the triangular shapes of cottonwood leaves. Maybe you didn't know you loved the smell of pine trees in the hot sun.*

4. From the times of the first cave artists, we have created out of our bodies. *Consider getting more closely in touch physically with your art. Try finger-painting, and feel the coolness of the color blue. Experience its slippery feel as you apply it to the paper. Do without your computer for a day and write with a yellow Number Two pencil. Dip leaves and grasses into mud and press them against paper. See the imprints they leave. Try this with your hands and feet.*

Chapter Five:
Wooing the Muse

Making the Muse Welcome

I am listening to the wind,
to the voice in the wind telling me
to write it all down. So I do.

—Kwame Dawes, *Wheels*

Do you have a muse? A person or an entity which you visualize or feel within yourself? Some one or thing that helps you along the creative path? Maybe it's a dream, a burning desire, a divine power which wants to work with you, through you, to bring a little more glory into the world. Maybe it's your most noble self, the way you are able to go on each day in the face of eventual mortality. Whatever it may be, we cannot help but benefit from being in league with a force which inspires and supports us, which urges us on in our creative work.

But sometimes, it seems, the muse is fickle. We may go through days of creative drought, the next great idea far away, out of reach. Shining sentences and astonishing paragraphs refuse to fall down on us as they did before. When this happens, we need to put out the welcome mat, be in a state of readiness—a pen or sketchbook in our hands, working. Let the muse peek into our windows and catch us sketching or doodling, and we might entice her to stop in and visit a while.

Stephen King sees his muse as male, and says of him that "he's not going to come fluttering down into your writing room and scatter creative fairy-dust all over your typewriter or computer station." Oh, if only that were true! "He lives in the ground," King says, "He's a basement guy. You have to descend to his level, and once you get down there you have to furnish an apartment for him to live in. You have to do all the grunt labor . . ."[39] In other words, we have to do the work—sit at our computers or with blank yellow legal pads in hand, and find a way for the words to come.

The beautiful Fanny Brawne is said to have been Keats' muse, and Shakespeare's a mysterious "Dark Lady." Once at a workshop, we asked writers to think about their sources of inspiration and draw sketches of these muses, however they perceived them. One drew a picture of a little girl, quiet, shy, but intense; another of a "crazy child" with wild hair, legs and arms gesturing dramatically. There was a drawing of ocean waves coming in to shore, lapping onto the sand; and another of a wild horse, rearing up on his hind legs, forelegs striking at the air. Maybe your muse has aspects of all these images—a little girl, a crazy child, the steady power of waves sweeping onto shore, and the high drama of a beautiful horse in all its force and majesty.

However we see the muse, and whether we believe in a muse or not, when we do our work faithfully day by day, a certain energy comes to us, surrounds us, and we are inspired. The key is to find ways to keep working, and in times of creative drought to be gentle with ourselves. Know that we have danced well before, have painted and written well, and will do so again. Take a walk in nature and be in solitude. Believe and the muse will come back to us. Woo the muse, be faithful to the gifts we have been given, and like the one who has always loved us, she will return.

---

[39] Stephen King, *On Writing* (New York: Scribner, 2000) 144.

Showers, Cows, What Else?

*The triumph of effective surprise is that it takes one
beyond the common ways of experiencing the world.*

—Jerome Bruner,
On Knowing: Essays For the Left Hand

It can happen to me in the shower. Creativity, that is, and it appears that I'm in good company, as a lot of folks, including Virginia Woolf, report that their best ideas often seem to come to them dripping wet. Woolf conceived her novel, *The Years*, as part of "a sudden influx of ideas" while bathing,[40] and Agatha Christie is said to have soaked in her Victorian tub, munching on apples as she dreamed up plot lines for her mystery novels. My friend Jude described how the inspiration for a neighborhood plan came to her while under a hot shower, the ideas flowing down on her from above.

Gertrude Stein had her own methods for finding inspiration, one of which involved driving around looking for cows. Cows? Apparently so. A 1934 *New Yorker* article described Stein and Alice B. Toklas, driving in the country, stopping at a likely spot, and Toklas with a switch or a stick "turning" a cow, adjusting its position so that her companion could see it. Then, if the cow suited that day's writing mood, Stein got out pen and paper and wrote for thirty minutes.

Recently, writing a piece on "Writing Productivity," which was failing to come together, I hopped on my bike and pedaled around the neighborhood, hoping to clear my head. Catching the wind, my jacket flapping, I sailed down a small hill when *whoosh!* Creative sparks began to ignite. I was *pedaling*, I thought, *cycling*. One word led to the

---

[40] Virginia Woolf, *The Diary of Virginia Woolf: Vol. IV, 1931-35*, ed. Anne Oliver Bell and Andrew McNeillie (London: Hogarth 1982).

next, from *cycling* to *cycle,* and then *season.* That was it, I realized. Writers experience different *cycles* with their productivity, different *seasons.* I'd write about that!

What do these three very different experiences have in common? Maybe jumping into a shower, driving around aimlessly, or bicycling provide the detachment needed for "effective surprise," as Jerome Bruner, American psychologist, describes.[41] Creativity, he states, can develop out of a combination of 1) commitment to a goal, and then 2) detachment from it, the "surprise" occurring during the detachment phase. At that time, while our minds and bodies no longer seem to be actively pursuing the goal, inwardly there remains an underlying commitment, the subconscious still working away towards a resolution. It's like receiving a personal note that requires a complicated answer, and putting it in your pocket. You know it's there, but you keep doing your errands. Then as Bruner describes, by putting yourself in a different perspective, the surprise moment comes, and you know what to say.

So, how might we tickle creativity, and enter into eureka moments more often? Engage in those activities that you enjoy. Bruner said to "keep an eye for the tinker shuffle, the flying of kites, and kindred sources of surprised amusement."[42] Wait and see if an idea or the next step for a project surfaces. Whatever happens, you'll enjoy the experience of doing what you like, and maybe something like a sudden rainstorm of ideas will come whooshing down.

---

[41] Jerome Bruner, *On Knowing: Essays For the Left Hand* (Boston: Belknap Press, 1979).

[42] Ibid.

The Quiet Side of Inspiration

I was quiet, but I was not blind.
—Jane Austen, *Mansfield Park*

Sometimes the spark of inspiration comes in dramatic fashion, astonishing us, nearly striking us down with its magnificence. Ruth Stone spoke of poems coming to her when she was outside working, the poem advancing "like a thunderous train of air" (as Elizabeth Gilbert relates) "barreling down at her over the landscape . . . " and she'd streak to the house to write it down before it thundered on by.[43] Brahms said that his ideas came to him on an undeviating path directly from God. William Blake, too, suggested that a goodly portion of his writing came as a result of "taking dictation."

Most usually, however, inspiration arrives more quietly, making its presence felt as a twinge or vague intimation, something on the fringe of consciousness. When it arrives subtly like this, it may be like the beam of a flashlight falling briefly on an object in the night. Though you catch a quick glimpse of that object, the light switches off again before you can quite make out what it might be. Sometimes flashes of creativity occur like this—just out of sight, out of reach. But there.

Psychologist William James defined stream of consciousness as images coming one after another, flowing as in a stream. Keeping that stream in mind, he describes subtle moments of inspiration like this: "Every definite image in the mind is steeped and dyed in the free

---

[43] Ruth Stone, qtd. in "Your Elusive Creative Genius," Elizabeth Gilbert, TED: Ideas Worth Spreading, 2009.

water that surrounds it."[44] In other words, the moment of illumination may *not* always come clear and bright and definite before us. We may not see it as we see a bright red leaf floating in the water. But if we pay attention, we may see the red reflection shimmering around it, the red stain—which had come about from the "steeping and dyeing" of the leaf, drifting from it. Sometimes creative ideas come at us slantwise, in a glimpse, something on the periphery, and if we do not pay attention, we'll miss them.

As artists and writers, the spark of inspiration is something over which we have little control. It comes when it comes. But we can pay heed to times when it presents itself in less than dramatic form—when it comes not like a lightning bolt striking down in front of you, but more like heat lightning, that faint glow far off in the distance.

Few of our best ideas come instantaneously, complete in structure, nuance, and complexity, but in vague inklings, hazy intuitions which must be developed. And while we still wait and hope for the dramatic, what we must do is to pay attention when inspiration appears more subtly, in twinges and nudges. Learn to honor them when they come, and recognize they may be the beginning of something fabulous, sublime.

[44] William James, *Principles of Psychology*, Vols. *1 & 2* (London: Macmillan, 1909).

The Smell of Remembering

*Already many of the memories of the previous two
weeks had faded: the smell of that small hotel in St.
Andrews; that mixture of bacon cooking for breakfast
and the lavender-scented soap in the bathroom; the air
from the sea drifting across the golf course; the aroma
of coffee in the coffee bar in South Street.*

—Alexander McCall Smith, *Trains and Lovers*

Have you ever encountered a smell that takes you back to a place
or person? A whiff of Old Spice, for instance, and you are a little
child sitting beside your grandfather at church. Or the sweet scent of
cinnamon and you're back in Aunt Mary's kitchen licking the bowl
while her head is turned. Smell triggers memory. As children, we
notice scents and associate them with certain people or experiences.
Years later, when we encounter the scent again, the same associations
are aroused and memories return.

Writers understand the power of details. As Natalie Goldberg
said, "This is not just my father; this is your father. The character who
smoked cigars and put too much ketchup on his steak."[45] We must care
about the details around us, using our senses to help us see and feel and
smell the world. And of the senses, scent is the one closely connected
to our most ancient neurosensory system, the limbic system, which is
concerned with intuition and long-term memory. It provokes heat and
energy, strong emotion, and can lead to vivid, powerful writing.

Every breath we draw is full of olfactory information, carrying
us across the fog of years and across miles delineated on a map. The

[45] Natalie Goldberg, *Writing Down the Bones: Freeing the Writer Within* (Boston: Shambhala Publications, Inc., 1986) 50.

scent of an apple orchard transports my husband and me to our favorite picnic area. I breathe in the heady smell of horse stables, and my old pinto, Diamond, comes galloping into view. One day, the whiff of peppermint delivered me to a beloved place of my youth.

In that instance, I was waiting in line in a country store where a huge display of old-fashioned candy was positioned close to the cashier. Brightly colored bins of candies adorned the aisle: wax-paper-covered caramels, toffees in red foil paper, and on the counter, striped red and white lollipops dressed up like dolls. A wonderful sweet, peppery scent came wafting through the air, and I was plunged back in time. Back to a small farmhouse with a sagging screened-in porch, my grandmother's home.

These images shine as brightly and vividly today as they did so many years ago, as if *now* is elastic and the poignancy of certain bygone events can easily rise to present awareness. These times of our lives are indelibly marked in our minds; and it may be the "scratch and sniff" of past experiences that gives rise to our words spilling magically on the page.

Sleep-Thinking

I dream my painting, and I paint my dream.

—Vincent van Gogh, qtd. in *Marry Your Muse:*
Making a Lasting Commitment to Your Creativity

Scientists delineate different levels of activity for the brain which correspond to different levels of consciousness, the brain producing beta waves when we are awake and alert, and alpha waves when we are at ease. It is in the time of alpha waves that most of our creativity takes place. When we are calm and relaxed, when we daydream.

Just as we have peripheral vision, observing by means of a sideways glance, or out of the corners of our eyes, it can also be said that we have a peripheral level of consciousness. We may call this a "twilight" level, when the beta waves of intense consciousness and thought give way to alpha waves. When the mind is in "idle" mode.

It is in this twilight state that remarkable things can happen. Maybe you have heard of writers who stumble out of bed and get to the page before they are fully awake. They are taking advantage of what may be described as "sleep-thinking," that relaxed state of mind where the subconscious holds sway and allows for the appearance of startling images and metaphors.

And when you are fully asleep? You go to bed with a problem on your mind, a decision to make, and awake knowing you have the solution. When you aren't actively attending to the issues before you, they often have a way of sorting themselves out. You decide to "sleep on it," and in the morning, you know what to do.

"Your waking brain is orderly," Jeffrey Kugler writes, "your sleeping brain is fragmented, and as with all broken things, the bits can get reassembled the wrong way. But 'the wrong way' suggests that there's just one way, and the genius of sleep is that it allows you to explore other, untried avenues."[46]

The Rolling Stones' guitarist Keith Richards had a habit of keeping a tape recorder by his bed so that if a song came to him in the middle of the night, he could record it. One morning he woke to find his recorder had wound to the end of the tape, though he didn't remember waking and doing any recording. He rewound the tape, played it back, and heard a three-note riff along with the mumbled words "I can't get no satisfaction." And he went on to write that song.

When we are asleep or nearly so, our thought processes work differently. Dreams are random, one dream morphing into the next, one seemingly ridiculous happenstance strangely linked to another. But it is in the strange associations, the untried avenues where creativity occurs. Where the odd, whoever-thought-of-that-connection becomes the just-right one.

We have been encouraged to wake up to our creativity. A better idea might be to relax, to sleep, and allow creativity to take place.

---

[46] Jeffrey Kugler, "How to Wake Up To Your Creativity," *Time*, April 30, 2017.

How the Song Sometimes Comes

Music is the shorthand of emotion.

—Leo Tolstoy, *The Live Corpse*

It is mysterious the way poems, stories, and songs sometimes come to us, popping up suddenly like a trout leaping from a stream to show its shining, glorious self a moment, before it disappears again into the water. But in that brief instant, we take in the beauty and wonder that is the trout. In the same way, there are times when, if we keep our minds open and our senses on alert, we will experience flashes of inspiration. An idea, a line or two of a poem or song will make itself known to us, and we have the opportunity to write it down.

One instance of this happened to me during a dark time in my life, the April my father died. Spring had taken its first baby steps, and the apple and cherry trees had begun to blossom, but after the funeral came several days when the temperature dipped below freezing. And every time I looked out the window, it was to see pink and white blossoms turning brown and fluttering to the ground, the newly blooming daffodils and tulips falling over to die. It seemed that everything around me was about sadness, and I slogged through each day, unable to find any peace or joy.

Still, there was something in me that wanted to be happy. One Saturday, driving west on the Interstate to see my mother, my mind on grief and trouble, a little mantra started in my head. "This is the day the Lord hath made, this is the day the Lord hath made." These words came from a refrigerator magnet a friend had given me, with the Bible verse, "Rejoice and be glad."[47] The words struck a chord, and as the

---

[47] Psalm 118:24. King James Version.

mantra repeated itself in my head, they did so to a little tune. More words came, and I found I was writing a song. I repeated the lyrics over and over so I wouldn't forget them, and at a rest area, called home on my cell phone and sang into the message machine. When my musician husband heard it, he was able to turn it into a song, one his bluegrass group includes regularly on their playlists.

I wish I could say that these dramatic moments of inspiration come on an everyday basis. They don't, at least not with as much pizzazz as they did that day on the Interstate. There are big, flashy miracles of inspiration that happen occasionally, and small sparks of light that shine on us almost every day. I like to depend on the bits of light that come dependably and regularly. When accumulated over a period of time, they can amount to an amazing collection of poems or songs.

Still, when I find myself driving alone on the Interstate, I keep hoping . . .

A Memory to Swear By

Memory . . . is the diary that we all carry about within us.

—Oscar Wilde,
The Importance of Being Earnest

With jet-like precision, taut as an arrow being shot, the big bird dives, and with a thud and a squawk, a red-tailed hawk lands on my brother's gloved hand. This is how memory happens, according to Mary Karr, with "a point of physical and psychic connection," the hawk's cry, the thump as he lands, and you have "a memory you'd swear by . . ."[48]

What was my brother's fascination with hawks? Was it a rite of passage to help him make the transition into the adult world? Nineteenth century falconers are said to have projected onto their hawks the masculine attributes they felt were in the process of disappearing— that of a man's ruggedness and vigor, his forcefulness and strength. For my brother in the 20th century, falconry may have provided a means to feel powerful, significant. The world was changing dramatically, but he and his friends still had their hawks.

Mary Karr said that a writer's biggest "lies" are in the area of "interpretation," and suggested that we be gentle and non-vindictive when describing others in our stories, to be as generous as we can.[49] I'm thinking about that now, trying to understand my younger brother Chuck's strange behaviors: trapping rodents and mail-ordering baby chickens as meals for his hawks. Now here, as I attempt to follow Mary Karr's advice, I find myself considering my brother's actions as merely baffling, odd, as opposed to crazy, *way out there,* or declaring,

[48] Mary Karr, *The Art of Memoir* (New York: Harper Perennial, 2015).
[49] Ibid.

as my cousin did, that he was "someone who needs to sleep in the barn."

As I was writing this piece, Chuck came to visit, so I asked about his hawk-flying days, and learned that he'd taken it up at an older age than I'd thought. Somehow, I'd seen him as an eleven-year old kid feeding frozen baby chicks to his wild birds. But he'd been fifteen. When I asked why he'd become absorbed in this particular passion, he didn't mention manhood or rites of passage. "Flying hawks was fun," my brother said. He swore by this. "Just something for Tom and me to do on a Saturday morning."

I don't know why this story sticks with me today. Maybe it's because I feel a little down, disappointed that my brother had such a pedestrian reason for flying hawks. But I should have known better. As Mary Karr suggested, "Anyone who wades deep into memory's waters drowns a little."[50] Or maybe it was something entirely different. Perhaps I was yearning for what we all wanted as children. When my brother was with his hawk, his feet did seem to lift off the ground.

---

[50] Ibid.

Making Lists Isn't Just for Santa

*The historian will tell you what happened. The novelist
will tell you what it felt like.*

—E.L. Doctorow, *Time*

Making lists can do surprising things for the mind. No, this isn't about bread, milk, and butter, but making lists to jumpstart your creativity. In *Zen in the Art of Writing,* Ray Bradbury described how making lists of nouns helped him generate new titles and ideas for stories. "These lists were the provocations, finally, that caused my better stuff to surface," he wrote. "I was feeling my way toward something honest, hidden under the trapdoor on the top of my skull."[51]

How does this work? It has to do with unsought connections, the association of words and images, and how the magic processes of the mind link these associations to particular feelings or emotions. For twenty-five years, Bradbury kept a sign over his typewriter that read, "Don't think," believing that he must *feel* his way towards what he put on the page, intuit the connections among the words he listed. For it is intuitive thinking which drives writing, he believed, and not the intellect, the intellect often working to *inhibit* creativity. On one of his lists, Bradbury included "circuses and carnivals," then remembered how terrified he was when his mother took him on his first merry-go-round ride. Many decades later, these images became part of his story, "Something Wicked This Way Comes."

When we make lists to stimulate creativity, we tap into our capacity for seeing patterns, revealing associations beneath "the trapdoors"

---

[51] Ray Bradbury, *Zen and the Art of Writing: Releasing the Creative Genius Within You*, (New York: Bantam, 1990).

of our skulls. It can be like finding that certain puzzle piece so that everything begins to fit together.

Why not try it? Make a list of the "firsts" in your life, things that make you cry, or flying objects. Or, make a list of things that scare you. Some time ago, I completed a list of *Things Which Frighten Me*, which included mice, loud noises, people with masks, spiders lurking in shoes, and wet basements. From these associations came my poem, "A Wolf Spider Speaks," about childhood, fear, and what might lurk in damp dark places.

A Wolf Spider Speaks

Standing like soldiers,
I see the cowboy boots
set to dry
in the far corner.

It's hard to find a home
on this cold slab of cellar,
nothing to burrow in,
nowhere to hang my web.

Now there's a perfect place,
the warm dark toe of the boot.
Actually, looking again,
I see there's room for two.

List-making serves to bring together seemingly disparate pieces of raw material from our minds; and when we review our lists and discover patterns, we see a certain underground intelligence at work. It's our intuition, giving us the insight to *feel* for the meaning and make sense of what is written. It's like the childhood game of hide-and-seek, feeling the joy when someone or something is found, oftentimes hidden in plain sight.

"Stand and Stare" Your Way to More Creativity

Boredom always precedes a great period of productivity.
—Robert M. Persig,
Zen and the Art of Motorcycle Maintenance

Perhaps you are familiar with current studies which suggest that boredom is necessary in nourishing the developing imagination of children. That young people need "stand-and-stare" time, and according to Dr. Teresa Belton, time alone with their thoughts and imaginings. We adults need that, too.

At night when we sleep, we rest, but the oxygen keeps coming in and out of our lungs, our amazing hearts keep moving red and white corpuscles throughout our bodies. And when we awake, we are re-energized and able to go about whatever is required of the new day. Similarly, standing and staring before the blank page or the blank canvas, or gazing out the window, we daydream, allowing our thoughts to be at rest. And just as sleep helps to reinvigorate our bodies, daydreaming serves to quicken the imagination. For what are we without the imagination? "The world of reality has its limits," Rousseau said, "but the world of the imagination is boundless."[52]

Therefore we must do what we can to nurture the imagination, to feed it what it needs, and oftentimes what it needs is "zoning out," daydreaming. The gears of our thinking processes grind to a halt, and what is left is a void, emptiness.

My friend Julie tells of listless summer afternoons as a child. She was alone a great deal, bored, without anything to do. Sometimes after lunch she sat on the porch and gazed out over the yard, not really seeing it, her mind empty. Gradually, her vision would come back into focus

---

[52] Jean Jacque Rousseau, *Emile* (1762).

and there was the garage, the doghouse, her father's shop, and the messy jungle of a place behind it. One day she found herself walking over to the shop where she began picking up sticks in the "jungle," clearing a space. She was making a playhouse, a secret schoolhouse, a hideout, happily following wherever her imagination took her.

What was happening here? "Boredom becomes a seeking state," according to psychologist Heather Lench.[53] Nature abhors a vacuum, and so does the mind. We get a little twitchy when ennui sets in. It's uncomfortable, dissatisfying when we have nothing to stir us, to occupy our thoughts. We are quick to pull out our cell phones to counteract any feelings of malaise. But if we resist that temptation and endure boredom a while, struggle with the discomfort, the brain can't help but work to do something about it. It is then that the creative new idea will come.

I am one who wants to be productive, to "get things done." But I'm longing for more stand and stare time, more dreaming time—for whatever new and wonderful thing may come into my life. Maybe this is something you would like, too.

---

[53] Heather Lench, qtd. by Clive Thompson, "How Being Bored Out of Your Mind Makes You More Creative," *Wired* (January 25, 2017).

Living Among the Glories

*It is the marriage of the soul with nature that makes
the intellect fruitful, and gives birth to the imagination.*

—Henry David Thoreau, *Journal*

We are what we eat, the old saying goes, and this is true, in that what we feed our bodies affects who we become as physical beings. Similarly, who we become spiritually and emotionally is influenced by what we feed *our souls.*

As a species, we evolved living in nature. We wandered the plains, tended plants and animals that shared the world with us, woke to majestic sunrises and watched in awe as the heavenly bodies crossed the skies. How did this all come to pass, we wondered. We flourished, breathing deep in the rhythms of the earth.

In our lives today, however, our connection with nature is more tenuous than it has ever been. Still, the natural world is there for us in all its dazzle and quiet beauty, and we depend upon it, we thrive upon it. "I go to nature to be soothed and healed," John Burroughs said, "and to have my senses put in order."[54] And Hans Christian Andersen said that "just living is not enough . . . one must have sunshine, freedom, and a little flower."[55]

We go for a walk and come back revitalized, refreshed. Even looking out a window to sky and trees beyond the glass can be restorative. Scientists have found that hospital patients with a garden view healed more quickly than those without, that students overlooking a green landscape performed better on tests than those in classrooms with no

---

[54] John Burroughs, *Studies in Nature and Literature* (Boston: Houghton, 1917).

[55] Hans Christian Anderson, *The Complete Fairy Tales* (New York: Random House, 1997).

windows, or only views of concrete. There is something about the serenity of green, of dappled sunlight and branches moving in the breeze. Our souls are hungry and nature nourishes us; we are troubled and it provides comfort.

My writing desk is situated so that I can see my garden. It doesn't face the garden, but I can turn my head and glance outside, see what clouds are moving across the sky, what juncos or sparrows are gathering at the feeder. Recently, when undergoing a renovation, I moved my study to the basement. My desk faced a wall, and I had only one small window at my back. As a result, my writing suffered. As did my mood. So I took my legal pad and pen and worked in longhand upstairs, went back down only to transfer what I'd written to my computer. I was able to breathe easily again, to write more freely.

Our surroundings matter, the milieu in which we conduct our lives. What we take in through our senses, the beauty of the earth. Walking in the verdant green or along great expanses of desert or water, we connect with the Divine and experience peace. We find the way to our best spiritual and emotional selves.

For Your Journey

She has the shimmer of a silver spoon, the elusiveness of a phantom, and a shape that fits. The Muse—she's everything to us. Our lover, inspirer, comrade-in-arms. We know we need her, but sometimes worry that our relationship is co-dependent. What can we do to make this relationship flourish?

We must court her, find out what she wants, bring her the gift of attention. Listen, then whisper in her ear. Know the Muse wants a relationship as much as you do. She is waiting.

1. Be willing to slow down and listen. *To stand and stare. Be willing to suspend certainty. To recognize novelty and creativity. Be willing to take a walk on a different path. Visit places outside your comfort zone. Be willing to honor ideas that pop into your head. Consider all ideas, even if they seem unworkable or a little crazy.*

2. Let your sense of smell lead you to an inspired destination. *Read the online poem, "Ode to the Belt Sander & This Cocobolo Sapwood" by Matthew Nienow. Make a list of the aromas or smells in which you have strong associations. Maybe it's the smell of newly mown hay. Old Spice and Grandfather. Think about the people, places or, perhaps animals that are associated with the scents you listed. Allow the aroma or smell to lead you to a drawing or a series of montages—whatever you want. Now create, breathing in this wonderful, scent-filled world.*

3. We know as artists and writers that if we are under a lot of stress, the shy Muse is hard to find. Our stuffed lives, air-conditioned

homes and offices, and long commutes may be contributing to our failure to do our art, to be the creative soul we long to be. In Japan, shinrin-yoku, a practice of forest bathing, was introduced several decades ago to promote a healthy lifestyle and reduce stress. Forest bathing—walking in nature—has a restorative quality and has been linked to improvements in "our senses, our emotions, our intellect, even our spirit," according to Dr. Stephen R. Kellert.[56] *Why not put on your walking shoes today? Get outside and surround yourself with trees and nature. You never know where the Muse may be hiding.*

4. The Muse likes to know she's welcome. Create rituals to help her feel at home. *Perhaps, lighting a candle and playing music are the sparks you need. Consider establishing a specific time of day to create, working with sunlight or walking in nature before you go to your studio. Constructing an altar to honor your Muse might encourage her to appear. For three weeks, assess with a plus or minus if certain environments are more productive for you. Acknowledge these for your future creative pursuits.*

[56] Stephen R. Kellert, "Children, Nature, and the Future of our Species (Giving Children the Gift of Nature)," *Biohabitats* 10, no. 4 (2012).

Chapter Six:
How the Magic Happens

Big Magic

. . . Poetry arrived
in search of me. I don't know, I don't know where
it came from, from winter or a river.
I don't know how or when . . .

—Pablo Neruda, "Poetry"

There's a certain excitement I feel when an idea is breaking through. It's as if I'm caught in a vortex swept up in an unknown force, pulled towards something unfathomable. Whatever it is, it is something good, something thrilling; and though I don't know where I'm going, I'm ecstatic, exhilarated, eager to follow wherever it takes me. I'm leaving the shadows, and ahead I see dappled light, then everything becomes clear. It is an idea, a marvelous one, and happily I take it in.

In *Big Magic*, Elizabeth Gilbert delves into the mystery of inspiration, stating that "our planet is inhabited not only by animals and plants and bacteria and viruses, but also by *ideas*."[57] And these ideas, she goes on to say, are driven by one powerful and all-consuming purpose: to be made manifest. But there is a hitch. Ideas are able to make their appearance *only* through the imperfect but creative genius of a human being. When an idea thinks you're a good person to bring it

---

[57] Elizabeth Gilbert, *Big Magic: Creative Life Beyond Fear* (New York: Riverhead Books, 2015) 34.

into the world, Gilbert suggests, it will tap you on the shoulder to get your attention.

Many times, however, you are too busy or distracted, and don't get the message. And the idea moves on to someone else. On the other hand, when you're relaxed and attuned to the world around you, the idea starts sending signals of inspiration, the universe collaborating with you to bring the idea into being. Planting coincidences in your path, surprising synchronicities to point you in the right direction. In the middle of the night, you'll wake thinking about the idea. As you read the newspaper or overhear conversations, it takes on deeper meaning, becoming fuller as it grows and takes form. And then, the idea will finally ask (according to Gilbert): "Do you want to work with me?"

When my youngest daughter was getting ready to leave for college, I found myself bombarded with a series of events that were, at first, unclear. I didn't know what was happening—I just kept getting all these "signals." A friend related to me over coffee how her son had changed since going off to college. For several nights, I awoke from recurring dreams about Canada geese flying south for winter— and getting lost. Then I spotted an ad in the paper announcing a new therapy series on *Letting Go*. The idea had finally gotten my attention, and I started to think about my daughter's leaving. I picked up my pen and wrote "The Empty Room," the poem appearing maybe not like *Big Magic*, but like water pounding again and again against the face of a dam, and finally bursting through.

The ideas for poems and stories are out there, somewhere in the vastness that is the universe. They are infinite in number, nebulous and unformed. They are waiting, perhaps for you, to pay attention to the tap on the shoulder and bring them into being.

Taking the Brain Out to Play

The creation of something new is accomplished not by the intellect but by the play instinct acting from inner necessity.

—Carl Jung, *Psychological Types*

If you were to draw a picture of the wind, what color would it be? Could you describe the smell of happiness? These are impossible kinds of questions—that is, when depending upon sheer intellect. But with a playful turn of mind, you might say that the wind is green. And that happiness smells the way a child does coming in from playing outside.

The brain is composed of white matter and gray matter, dendrites, axons, and neurons. It's the most complex organ in the body, and we work it hard. We depend upon it to keep us alive, perform complicated linguistic and mathematical tasks, make decisions and judgments, and take in the world and muse about it. It is also the birthplace of creativity.

In the 1990s, neurologist Marcus Raichle undertook research to study the mind at work. Interested in pinpointing areas of the brain involved in specific activities such as reading aloud, say, as opposed to reading silently, he attached test subjects to a brain scanner and recorded which areas of the brain "lit up" for each particular activity. And in between tasks, in order to establish a baseline, the subjects were instructed to relax, to let their minds go blank.

What he found was a surprise. When the brains were supposedly idle, they were anything but. Instead, they lit up with all kinds of activity. The subjects were "at ease," not needing to be focused on any particular task, and when they had the opportunity, they indulged in daydreaming, playing around in their minds. It's remarkable: when a muscle is at rest, it rests, but when a brain is at rest, *it plays*, wondering about the future, thinking about things like how the word *winter* rhymes with *bitter*, the sound wind makes as it blows through telephone wires. Or what it might have been like living in the 1800s during a bitter cold winter with no television or telephones. In other words, the "lazy" brain, the brain in its "default" state, is far from idle. It is busy making connections, setting the groundwork for whatever issues (including creative issues) lie before us.

We may think of the brain as functioning like a computer, or like a mathematics instructor working out on a whiteboard the logical and inevitable solution to an algebra problem. In some cases, the brain may indeed work that way. But there are things of the world for which logic doesn't apply—art and its companions of creativity and innovation. It is in *associations* made by the mind, the brain playing around, that exciting new ideas are born. Henri Matisse said: "Creative people are curious, flexible, persistent, and independent with a tremendous spirit of adventure and love of play."[58] We know it is important to spend time working, focused on our creative projects. But we must also allow unfocused time for our thoughts to meander, to give ourselves over to play.

---

[58] Henri Matisse, "Notes of a Painter," *La Grande Revue* (25 December 1908).

Cross-Training

Around here, we don't look backwards for very long.
We keep moving forward, opening new doors and doing
new things, because we're curious . . . and curiosity
keeps leading us down new paths.

—Walt Disney, *Meet the Robinsons*

Many of my friends are great at pursuing their fitness goals—they walk or run, swim, lift weights, choosing activities which appeal to them and help achieve results. What keeps them going, they report, is that they participate in a *variety* of pursuits. One might decide to run four days a week, and lift weights two. Then if running becomes too routine (or if shin splints or sore knees present a problem) they substitute swimming or biking. The idea, of course, is that the objective is *fitness*. Cross-training—choosing other activities that keep you interested—and which work different muscles—can help you reach your goal.

My musician husband is a strong adherent of cross-training—not only in regards to staying in shape, but in becoming a better musician. He started playing guitar and banjo in his mid-forties, and did pretty well—taking lessons, practicing at least an hour a day, and joining in jam sessions to help him reach higher levels of musicianship. But it wasn't until he took up the mandolin, he says, that his playing really took off. "The mando stretched me, opened my mind to different musical concepts," he explains, "so that stringing licks together was no longer a matter of rote memory. I knew intuitively what to do."

For athletes, musicians, and all of us in our creative lives, cross-training can be invaluable in stretching our abilities, creating more *aha!* moments, and helping us develop as artists. If you are a visual

119

artist working in pen and ink, try watercolors. Or oil, or collage. If you are a poet, consider writing essays or short fiction. Writer and friend Mary Kay Stillwell advises that when we have a poem that just won't work, we should "ask if it would feel more comfortable as a short story or memoir," and go on to write the piece that way. Not only will this result in completed work, but when we write in areas which are not necessarily our forté, we become stronger all around.

To take this a step further, consider short story writer and musician, Luke Hawley. When Luke gets stuck in the middle of a piece of short fiction, he takes a break from it, and instead writes a *song* about one of the characters or the setting he's writing about. This enables him to find a new way into the piece, helps him take a different view. Then, he is able to go on and successfully complete the story.

"There are a hundred ways to kiss the ground," Rumi said,[59] and ultimately, that is what creativity is about. Exploring new paths in the search for beauty and truth, finding new ways to love the world.

[59] Rumi, "Spring Giddiness," *The Essential Rumi* (San Francisco, CA: Harper, 1996).

Hitting Rock Bottom

There is a kind of despair we feel as writers and artists
that is not only useful, but necessary.

—Dani Shapiro, *"On Productive Despair"*

In 1965 Bob Dylan, just back from an exhausting European tour, felt that his love affair with music was over. There was no joy in his work; his performances felt canned, without energy, his creative drive missing. "I was going to quit singing," he said. "I was very drained and the way things were going, it was a very draggy situation."[60]

There are varying accounts of exactly what happened next, but at the conclusion of the tour, "in all likelihood," according to *Gaslight Records*, he headed to the little cabin he and his wife rented in Woodstock, New York, and continued work on lyrics to a new song he'd started in Europe. He described what he'd written as "this song, this story, this long piece of *vomit* twenty pages long."[61] And from that came the signature piece for his *Highway 61, Revisited* album, "Like a Rolling Stone," a song that revolutionized rock music.

Such a breakthrough came after a long period of dissatisfaction, of not being able, as Dylan said, to "dig" himself. Sometimes, it seems, you have to hit rock bottom, let despair wash over you, and accept that your art isn't working. Accept defeat. And then? After we've *let go,* something new comes into our brains, into our worlds, and we discover what we've been looking for.

Maybe you've had this experience too. Perhaps you have to say a few words for a friend at a going away party but nothing seems quite

---

[60] Bob Dylan, qtd. by Sam Pethers in "June 14th, 1965: Bob Dylan writing 'Like A Rolling Stone,'" *Gaslight Records*.
[61] Ibid.

right. You work and work, getting nowhere, and finally, frustrated, you give up and go to bed. And as soon as your head hits the pillow, the words come.

It would be wonderful, wouldn't it, if we didn't have to go through the frustration, the sometimes agony? Why can't the insight come right away? Without going down the seemingly endless wrong paths, without the time of sitting and staring at the blank page? Well, sometimes it *does* come easily. Often, however, one of the requirements of creativity seems to be a long walk down the wrong road, hours of effort with what appear to be no result. As Dani Shapiro writes, despair can be useful, and oftentimes, it's *necessary.*[62]

The secret is that the hours of effort aren't really wasted. It's like you're in your car stuck in a snow drift. You back up and go forward a little; your wheels start to spin, so you back up and give it another go. And another go again. You rock back and forth and eventually blast out of the drift. We can blast out of creative droughts too. Try a new tack, get a new perspective, take a break when you need to, and the good work will come.

---

[62] Dani Shapiro. "On Productive Despair," *DaniShapiro.com* (July 30, 2017).

The Way of Epiphanies

Small things can start us off in new ways of thinking.
—V. S. Naipaul, *A Bend in the River*

Remember the feeling that comes when you finally understand? When you come face to face with an essential truth that has—until now—eluded you? It may be something complex like comprehending a concept in technology; or profoundly simple, like realizing you are in love. Whatever the specifics, these epiphanies, sudden insights, or perceptions, are thrilling the moment you suddenly understand—that you "get it."

One well-known epiphany is that of Archimedes sitting in his bathtub and discovering the principle of the displacement of water. Or Newton being struck by a falling apple, and from that experience going on to develop the theory of gravitation.

Each of us has what we might call "little" epiphanies more often than we realize. They can come about when we find the right word for a crossword puzzle or solve a brain teaser. Or when we suddenly realize truths about the world and about ourselves. Maybe you discover that your family likes the simple cake you whip up more than the elaborate dessert that takes half the day to prepare. Or that the most enjoyable moments of your day come when you are outside.

Writers experience lots of small epiphanies—finding the right word, the right plot twist, how to frame the conclusion of the short story. As do photographers, discovering the magic of certain types of light, different approaches to portraiture. Epiphanies can be magical, life-changing. For when we have an epiphany and realize a new truth, we can act upon it. And that can have lasting impact on our art and our lives.

But how can we experience epiphanies more often? In her book, *Snap*, psychologist Katherine Ramsland writes that for epiphanies to occur, several conditions must exist. We must have experience in a certain area, be presented with a challenge in that area of expertise, struggle to meet the challenge, which must be difficult but achievable, and then surrender.[63] Consider again, Archimedes in his bathtub, Newton reclining beneath an apple tree. After sustained effort, a time of relaxation—or if you will—capitulation.

There are times we consciously strive for a solution to a problem, and at other times, it occurs beneath the surface of conscious thought. And what we discover may be astonishing, life-changing. "Sometimes the dreams that come true," Alice Sebold wrote, "are the dreams you never even knew you had."[64] These are often the best dreams of all.

---

[63] Katherine Ramsland, *Snap: Seizing Your Aha! Moments* (New York: Prometheus Books, 2012).

[64] Alice Sebold, *The Lovely Bones* (New York: Little, Brown, 2002).

A Country Without Borders

If the doors of perception were cleansed, everything
would appear to man as it is, infinite.

—William Blake, *A Memorable Fancy*

Whether it's new countryside or familiar ground we're exploring, when we tap into the use of metaphor and simile, we move away from the tried and true to a place where an early morning stubble field is transformed into the Mohave Desert, where a tomato-shaped pincushion becomes a dwelling for a family of fairies. Finding these ingenious connections, we add delight to our lives. What once may have gone by unnoticed becomes distinct, relevant. We see the familiar with new eyes, as when my friend Jude described the hindquarters of our yellow Labrador as "the backside of a linebacker in a tight jersey."

Tapping into the imagination is like throwing a many-sided die. Each time we roll, it leads us in another direction, gives us another angle, our imaginations transporting us anywhere—to the Klondike piloting a dogsled, picking cotton in Georgia, or sailing majestically on the Blue Danube. We set aside some aspects of ourselves in order to open to others, taking off our heavy boots and walking lighter, or swapping the burdens of worry and frustration for hope.

How can we move away from the tried and true? Robert Frost wrote that when "Two roads diverged in a yellow wood," he chose "the one less traveled by / And that has made all the difference."[65] Why *not* take that road? Why not let the magic of imagination take us on grand adventures? When we do, it's not the road that makes the

---

[65] Robert Frost, "The Road Not Taken," *Mountain Interval* (New York: Henry Holt and Company, 1916) 9.

difference but the experiences we encounter along the way. We trade our universe, momentarily, for another.

We all have things in our heads that no one else has. Try throwing a leaf in the air and following its path on the way down. Let the whimsy of the wind blow you in new directions and cleanse your "doors of perception," removing old cataracts, and beholding the world with new-found innocence. Then, the infinite capacities of the universe show their multi-faceted faces, and a new country, one without borders, stretches wide and open before us.

In "Song of Myself," Walt Whitman didn't see boundaries within, describing his "self" as a universal self, one of the fraternity of humanity and God. He connected with all—men and women, those in different walks of life, and even animals. He wrote of himself as a "gigantic beauty of a stallion," "both old and young." "I am large," he said, "I contain multitudes."[66]

We can step into other worlds through our art, our writing. Let the walls around you disappear for a while and find that marvelous place with no borders to hold you back.

---

[66] Walt Whitman, "Song of Myself," *Leaves of Grass*, (New York: Doubleday Publishing, 1855).

Nighttime Dreams: Creative Wonderland

I know that if we meditate on a dream sufficiently long
and thoroughly, if we carry it around with us and turn
it over and over, something almost always comes of it.

—Carl Jung, *The Practice of Psychotherapy*

Have you ever awoken with a start from a nighttime dream that offered possibilities or potential solutions to a creative problem? Insight into a story you're writing, perhaps, or the perfect words to finish your poem? In *Writers Dreaming* by Naomi Epel, Maya Angelou said that dreams can help us work out our problems, including our creative ones. How? "The brain says, 'Okay, you go to sleep,'" Angelou explained, and "'I'll take care of it.'"[67]

Epel goes on to say that many other writers from the past century— John Cheever, Doris Lessing, Edgar Allan Poe, Stephen King, and more—have also recognized the power of dreams, using images and words arising during sleep as inspiration. When we pay attention to our dreams, we tap into the intuitive part of the mind, which is not just about problem-solving, but providing insights to guide us along our creative paths.

Several years ago, a friend shared with me a recurring dream she had—images of a small child in a pink dress who kept wandering about and getting lost. For a long time, she was puzzled. What did the dream mean? At last, in a lightning strike of recognition, she understood. "All the pressures of family, work, and living were hindering my creativity," she told me. "The lost child was my creative self which wanted to be found, calling to me, asking, *where am I in your life?*"

---

[67] Maya Angelou, qtd. by Naomi Epel, *Writers Dreaming: 26 Writers Talk About Their Dreams and the Creative Process* (New York: Vintage Books, 1994).

Dreams open doors of all colors, shapes, and sizes, sometimes taking us through ancient portals to an inner world. They allow us to break away from the occupied workday mind, the rational mind, stirring ideas that we never thought possible. Dreams have inspired me to write about subjects that are far from the patterns of my daily life. I've written about a red-haired Irishman with one arm, a gravedigger, a mosque, and stardust. Countless other fascinating topics and themes I never would have come up with in my wide-awake world.

The impulse to create our first book, *Writing in Community,* came from a nighttime dream in which my writing partner, Lucy Adkins, and I were writing together composing a manuscript. In it, we told sparkling stories of the writing process at work, provided writing prompts and examples of writings which came about as a result. It was a meaningful and exciting idea. When I shared it with Lucy, we went to work, following the advice of author and scholar Harry Edwards— *to dream with our eyes open.* Four years later, the book which began as a dream, had a life of its own.

The Hallway of Tapestries

You use a glass mirror to see your face; you use works of art to see your soul.

—George Bernard Shaw, *The She-Ancient*

Once my husband and I were so fortunate as to travel to Italy, experience the culture there, the beauty of the country and its people, and see some of the works of art that until that time I had only read about. One event that stood out was visiting the city of Rome and the Vatican. We saw sculptures and paintings, the haunting beauty of the Pieta, the magnificence of the Sistine Chapel—beauty and artistry beyond imagining.

Then we followed our tour guide to the Hallway of Tapestries. "On one side of the hall," she told us, "are works of excellent craftsmanship, the colors just right, the weaving perfect, good work—but not art. And on the other side are tapestries which are masterpieces." She paused to let us consider. "Which is which?" she asked. "And how can you tell?"

Our group looked from side to side—at images of the Nativity, Jesus and his disciples on a fishing boat in the Sea of Galilee, the Last Supper—and remained silent—unable or unwilling to hazard a guess. "Look at the eyes," the guide suggested. And then we knew. In the tapestries in which the eyes were liquid with emotion, we saw works of art. Works that made us draw in our breath, stopped us in our tracks.

How does this happen? Why is it that some efforts at the loom resulted in tapestries alive with humanity—and some did not? And why is it that some of our writing takes wing and soars—and at other times it flies a little way and then drops to the ground?

We want to be the best we can be. We want to be Anita Shreves or Ernest Hemingways or Georgia O'Keeffes. It is the extraordinary we strive for. But we cannot agonize about perfection. We just need to work, to put down one sentence after another, knowing that on some days, a good sentence or two will be enough. A line or two of a poem. We need to be like the turtle, slow and steady, faithful to the process, trying to develop our craft. For we *must* be good craftsmen—continue to learn and develop in our writing, read other good writers and glean what knowledge we can from them.

All of our efforts will not be Art—that is, art with a capital A, but we keep at it. Then one day out of nowhere a line will come, a paragraph, a verse or two of poetry that goes beyond expert craftsmanship. "The muse is looking for someone with a pen in her hand," my friend told me once. It comes when we are working at our writing desks. It also comes when we are on a walk or mowing the lawn, when we least expect. So we keep on, doing what we can every day to become better writers. And on some days, we will make Art.

Like a Child

You have to ask children and birds how strawberries and cherries taste.

—Author Unknown

Sometimes I think that the most productive and satisfying way we can write is to do so in as childlike a manner as we can. For what do children do? They play. They line blocks up one on top of another, create playhouses behind the garage, make castles and moats in their sandboxes. And do they care if the blocks are lined up by color? If the playhouse has dirt floors? No, of course not. Nor do they care if the turret on the castle is a little crooked. Children absorb themselves in the world of the imagination, putting all their heart and soul and energy into what they are doing. Playing is serious business in that children devote their full attention to it, but at the same time it's not. Kids at play have fun. They giggle and laugh, delighting in the funny angle of the castle wall, the way the blocks fall down. They just play. Then they have a snack and a story and take a nap. And when they wake up, they play some more.

I like the idea of writing in this same way. Picasso said, "it took me four years to paint like Raphael, but a lifetime to paint like a child,"[68] and Thomas Hardy suggested that "the secret of genius is to carry the spirit of childhood into maturity."[69] But this is easier said than done. Oftentimes we writers make writing too much work. We get too

---

[68] Pablo Picasso, qtd.by Marina Picasso, *Picasso, My Grandfather* (New York: Riverhead Books, 2001).

[69] Thomas Hardy, qtd. by Peter Selgin, *By Cunning & Craft: Sound Advice and Practical Wisdom for Fiction Writers* (New York: F+W Media, 2007).

serious, agonizing over every word, and when we do that, we freeze up. In the infant stages of new writing, we just need to write, jotting down whatever odd thing comes to mind, making whatever crazy connections we want. Our writing is our sandbox, our tower of blocks, our playhouse behind the garden shed.

Children were intended to play, to mess around, to try this and try that and see what works. We human beings (adults, too!) were made to create and to have a good time doing it. And when we allow ourselves to loosen up and let the crazy, quirky, childlike part of our selves make itself known through the scratching of our pens, we do our best writing.

To Reach Excellence: Quantity vs. Quality

You've got what it takes, but it will take everything you've got.

—Conscious Magazine

What would you rather have? Two or three true blue friends? Or thirty or forty casual acquaintances? Would you rather write *one* beautiful compelling story or *five* stories that are just so-so? I think that most of us would prefer a few true friends we can share anything with, friends with whom we can have deep meaningful relationships—over having scores of acquaintances that never approach this level of closeness. As writers, we value quality—preferring to write something truly good—maybe even great—as opposed to more works that are not up to the mark. The trick is . . . how do you do that? You meet a number of people before you find those who become your soulmates. And you need to write a great deal before you become an accomplished writer.

Recently a songwriting friend, a scientist, told me about a study regarding the creative process involved in writing new songs. In a group of twenty songwriters, each was given twelve hours to write the *best* song he could, and another group of twenty were each to use the twelve hours to write as *many* songs as possible. At the end of this time period, which group produced the songs that were the most touching, most memorable, the kind of songs that had the potential to become truly great? The results were surprising. The best songs came from the group focusing on *quantity.*

As writers, what can we learn from this? Some things we probably already know: that the intent and ability to reach excellence is within, but we cannot force it. It comes when it will, and it comes most easily when we write freely, joyfully, and when we write a great deal. It

133

comes not from waiting for inspiration or the perfect concept or perfect sentence to float into our minds, but by turning off our internal editors and going after inspiration. Just writing.

"If I waited for perfection," Margaret Atwood said, "I would never write a word."[70] Julia Cameron advises us to "take care of the quantity and let God take care of the quality."[71] So, we must do that, take care of the quantity. Bring in the world with all its flurry, excitement, imperfection, and write with abandon. Let creativity have her way.

---

[70] Margaret Atwood, "A Progressive Interview With Margaret Atwood" by Matthew Rothschild, *The Progressive*, December 2010.

[71] Julia Cameron, *The Artist's Way* (New York: Tarcher-Perigee, 1992).

For Your Journey

Creativity is a mysterious thing. There is no formula for it, no scientific explanation, no reasoned-out plan to put the imagination into play. You can't say to yourself: o*kay, I'm going to sit down now and be creative,* and expect great poems or ideas to spring forth instantaneously. Creativity is a lot like love. You don't *will* it into being; it just happens. And like love, when it happens, it's wonderful. There are, however, certain conditions under which creativity is more likely to take place.

1. "Make an empty space in any corner of your mind," Dee Hock said, "and creativity will instantly fill it."[72] So, in order to nurture our creative souls, we must not only allot time to work on our art, we must plan for more "empty" time in our lives—sitting on a park bench or at the living room window, staring outside. *We must take leisurely walks and leisurely baths. Don't feel that in these moments you must be purposely looking for special images or concocting plots or ideas for paintings. Just let thoughts and word pictures float into and out of your mind.*

2. For a month or more, keep a dream journal, every morning jotting down an account of your dreams, whether they be dream fragments or full-fledged dreams with beginnings, middles, and endings. *Then on a weekly or monthly basis, go back and read your dream journal, taking note of any recurring themes that provide insight or lead to new perspectives. Do your dreams suggest any changes you should consider? Any*

---

[72] Dee Hock, qtd. by Mitchell Waldrop, "Dee Hock on Management," *Fast Company*, October/November 1996. https://www.fastcompany.com/27454/dee-hock-management.

acts of creativity you could try? From time to time before you go to sleep, say to yourself: "I'm going to use my dreams to inform my art tomorrow." What associations can you make to extend or enhance your creativity? For puzzling dreams, consider "drawing" your dream, giving it form and color.

3. Where does your art come from? A Divine Power? The universe, or some other mysterious source? *Put on some soothing music—perhaps the Celtic music of Enya or that of Relativity, and reflect upon the intangibles of your art. Close your eyes, relax, and allow images to float through your mind. What do you see? Stars, the great expanse of the universe, the idea of wind? Something concrete or abstract? Then using paints or markers, create a representation of what you feel might be the source of your art, from where or whom it comes.*

4. Indulge in your senses. *Plan a day to take in the sounds of the world around you. Notice the gurgling of your coffeemaker, the clicking of the cardinal on your morning walk, the rustling of the leaves. Take note of the calls of children at the elementary school, the growl of a delivery truck. Do the same with the other senses—that of smell, touch, taste, and sight. Check out from the library a book of the art of Frida Kahlo or Cezanne or Georgia O'Keefe. Study them, become a little obsessed. Go to an art gallery and let the colors and patterns wash over you, the pictures suggest stories. Then buy postcards to take home with you—let that which is beautiful and intriguing surround you.*

PART THREE:
THE VILLAGE

Being human, we are imperfect. That's why we need each other. To catch each other when we falter. To encourage each other when we lose heart.

—Hillary Clinton,
addressing the Democratic Convention

Chapter Seven:
The Village

The Loneliness of the Artist

Writing is a solitary occupation, and one of its hazards is loneliness.

—Joyce Carol Oates, *A Widow's Story*

Some of the best times of your writing life come with long hours of uninterrupted work, a story unspooling before you on the computer screen, becoming one with the characters, the words flowing freely. But then the writing day comes to an end and you look up from your work, feeling strange, disconnected. As if you don't know where you belong.

What's going on here? More than likely, it is loneliness you're feeling, a longing for meaningful connection, the kind of lonely which is different from being in solitude. You want to talk to someone who will understand that you can spend all day finding your way into a new chapter. Someone to despair with when you're blocked.

This is where the writing community comes in, the communities of artists and musicians: people you meet at art exhibits or at poetry and literature festivals, in art classes and writing retreats and music camps. Those who know the world you live in, and who "get" what you're doing. And since an individual's art is intense and personal, the relationships you develop among those in that community can be as ardent, as fervent as romantic relationships.

Painters Vincent van Gogh and Paul Gauguin developed such a

relationship. Not a romantic one, but a close artistic friendship. They lived together for a time, painted together and learned from each other. Other well-known artistic friendships include poets Elizabeth Bishop and Robert Lowell, and novelists James Baldwin and Toni Morrison. Great relationships come when you share your life. And when a great part of that life is your music or sculpture or acting, it's important to have someone who can comprehend the highs and lows of that life. Someone who will ask: *How is your writing going? Your painting?* And realize that the answer reveals how it is *you* are doing, how it is with your soul.

"An artist is always alone—if he is an artist," Henry Miller said. And then he corrected himself. "No, what the artist needs is loneliness."[73] Writing or painting or composing music requires long stretches of focus and concentration, withdrawal from the world. It's a strange irony: we need solitude, alone time to create that which brings meaning and purpose; but the meaning can fall a little flat without someone to share it with. We must be of the world to create art, but at the same time, we must be apart. How can we do that?

The answer is that we must find people who will help us flourish, our artistic close kin, our writing tribe. They are out there, lonely like we are, wanting someone who understands, just as we do. We must find one another.

---

[73] Henry Miller, *The Rosy Crucifixion I: Sexus* (New York: Grove Atlantic, Inc., 1949).

Roses, The Impressionists, and Writing Groups

We are a species that gathers into community, not just
we the writer species, but we the human species.

—Judy Reeves, *A Writer's Book of Days*

A few years ago, on a trip to France, I visited Claude Monet's beautiful home and garden in Giverny. What I remember most about the visit was Monet's second-story bedroom overlooking his rose garden. Two floor-to-ceiling windows faced the south, and I imagined Monet in May and June and July rising early, going to the windows and flinging them open to the roses below. How could he not help but paint as he did, I thought, waking to such beauty every morning?

After that visit, I became intrigued with the impressionists, going to every exhibit of their work I could find, lugging home stacks of art books from the library. One book that particularly interested me was Sue Roe's *The Private Lives of the Impressionists*, which describes how the painters banded together to encourage, support, and learn from one another. Cezanne was a frequent guest at Pissarro's home in Pontoise where the two sketched and painted together; Renoir, Bazille, and Monet took train trips from Paris Sunday afternoons to paint *en plein aire* (in the open air); and at one time, Renoir and Monet shared a studio. These painters, in various groupings and configurations, made great leaps in their development as individual artists, and through their work as a whole, made dramatic changes in the world of art.

How similar those relationships must have been to ones found in writing communities today. We all need encouragement. Sometimes we need a little nudge to keep going, and we need the companionship of other writers, people who not only understand the challenges of the writing life, but who can suggest new possibilities and help us grow.

141

The Fire Inside

Nowhere is this more powerful, we feel, than in the generative writing group, sometimes known as the "writing practice group." In this type of group, writers gather together, a writing prompt is shared, and then there is silence except for the scribbling and scratching of pens. "Writing may be a solitary endeavor," Judy Reeves wrote, "but what writer couldn't use a little support, feedback, and camaraderie?"[74] The generative group provides this, and just as Renoir and Monet most usually had a new painting after the end of a day of painting together, so do writers at the end of a writing group session have a new poem or the beginnings of a short story.

We may not have a home in France (though we can dream!) or a second story window to gaze out upon a rose garden, but we can have the inspiration of a writing group to spark new ideas and generate new work, whether this be a gathering of five to twelve that meets regularly, or the occasional writing session with a comrade at a coffee shop. We all get by, as we know—in fact, we thrive—with a little help from our friends.

---

[74] Judy Reeves, *Writing Alone, Writing Together*, (Novato: New World Library, 2010).

Standing on the Shoulders

*All creators, even the most celebrated ones, draw on
the work of others, influenced consciously or not . . .*
—Richard Jerome, *The Science of Creativity*

Everything we hear and see influences our creative efforts. We may not recognize this, however, until the moment an image floating in the ether arrives at its destination on the page or unfolds in a sketch before us. As if it had been waiting for that very moment. And most likely that idea or image *had* been waiting, according to neuroscientist Anthony Brandt and composer David Eagleman. They describe how the brain continually works the "sensory data it receives," transforming "the fruit of that labor [into] new versions of the world."[75] All creative ideas evolve, they believe, from one or more of three interactive processes, that of *bending, breaking* and *blending*. In drawing on the work of others—whether consciously or not—we reconfigure existing ideas and forms to make our own creations.

It sounds complicated, and taking into consideration the complex but quiet work of the brain, it is. But by tapping into these processes, we can extend our abilities, recombining and reassembling what we've seen and heard to create new turns of phrase, musical scores, and concepts for photography.

Brandt and Eagleman describe *bending* as the process of modifying or twisting the original out of shape. As when my young friend Mollie created her first public art exhibit. She had long admired certain features of homes she'd visited, and remembering bits and attributes of this and that room, created miniature versions of rooms complete

---

[75] Anthony Brandt and David Eagleman, "Under the Hood of Creativity," *Time: The Science of Creativity*, August 3, 2018.

with tiny wall hangings and doll furniture she crafted herself. Then she photographed the resulting mini-rooms and transformed them into prints. She *bent* the original and made it her own work.

The creative process of *breaking* began for me one morning with the radio playing Greg Brown's "Our Little Town." "What's going to happen to our little town?" he sang. The song stuck in my mind, and later, sitting down to write, the phrase took me deeper into thinking about *my* own small town: the brick boulevard, corner grocer, the empty storefronts on Main Street. "They say it's dying though and there ain't a thing we can do."[76] I began considering the instances of loss I'd encountered, not only in regards to the town of my childhood, but all loss, the passing of time, and decline. Writing, I broke the words and emotions apart, and from the fragments, created an essay detailing my own experiences, what had once been in my life and now was gone.

The last of the three elements, *that of blending,* according to Brandt and Eagleman, "combines two or more sources in novel ways to form something different."[77] In ancient Greece, mythology told of a being which was part-man and part-bull—a Minotaur. Another example is that of kinetic art, which creates movement or the *impression* of movement through the blending of multiple materials, as in the metal "man" waving at me from the park entrance, created from a mélange of old bicycle parts and garden tools.

Perhaps when we feel all alone as artists, we should step back for a moment. Let's imagine we are hooking arms with all those creative souls who came before— all of us chasing down slivers of inspiration, sharing, reconfiguring, and making them our own.

---

[76] Greg Brown, "Our Little Town," track 10 on *One More Kiss Goodnight*, Red House, 1988, compact disc.

[77] Anthony Brandt and David Eagleman, "Under the Hood of Creativity," *Time: The Science of Creativity*, August 3, 2018.

Sometimes, It Takes Two

Creativity is just connecting things.

—Steve Jobs, qtd. in *Wired*

Ah, love—it pulls at you, turns you to putty; it opens you up and leaves you exposed and tingling with what it means to be alive. It's wonderful and terrible. When two artists are lovers as well as creative partners, the relationship can be fiery, each playing his or her role as lit matches—encouraging, inspiring, and exhorting one another to higher reaches of creativity. Such was the case with photographer and art dealer, Alfred Stieglitz, and artist Georgia O'Keeffe. O'Keeffe was the first female modernist, an American artist of flowers and of the southwestern landscape, who expressed her deepest emotions through painting. When asked to describe her art, however, she had difficulty doing so. "Words and I are not good friends," she said.[78] Stieglitz, her lover and eventual husband, described her flower paintings as being about femininity, sexuality, and the female body. He brought her to New York, set up a show for her, and was instrumental in bringing her to the attention of the art world.

In turn, O'Keeffe's influence on Stieglitz's art was similarly profound. After first meeting her, his artistic career (which he'd put on hold) began to take off. He wanted to take photographs—of her—and in "a kind of heat and excitement," he did. "I am at last photographing again," he confided to a friend. "It is straight. No tricks."[79] For the next two decades he devoted a great part of his artistic energies to

---

[78] Alfred Stieglitz to Sadakichi Hartmann, Apr. 27, 1919, Alfred Stieglitz/Georgia O'Keeffe Archive, Yale Collection of American Literature, Beinecke Rare Book and Manuscript Library, Yale University, box 23, folder 546.

[79] Ibid

creating portraits of Georgia O'Keeffe. It was some of his best and most famous work.

We'll never know the degree to which Stieglitz and O'Keeffe impacted one another, but we do know—from the outpouring of their art and from the 25,000 pages of correspondence between the two—that each became a greater artist due to their relationship. They grew, explored new territory, and created opportunities for each other, their personal and creative interconnections helping to lead them to pre-eminence in their respective fields.

Stieglitz and O'Keeffe are not alone. We all are aware of similar partnerships—musicians, writers, or other artists—couples who share romantic passions as well as creative ones, and whose careers are greater due to the support and inspiration of the other. Maybe *you* belong to one of these pairings.

Not all romantic-creative relationships, however, work well. No one is perfect. Partners can become critical or jealous, dampening the spirit of the other, ultimately impacting their creativity. In a collaboration, finding the right partner is essential. And as dynamic as it might be, a romantic partner, of course, is not a prerequisite for working together effectively, but only a deep commitment to the work. As authors of this book, we have been collaborators for ten years, co-writing first of all, *Writing in Community*, and now *The Fire Inside*. When asked how we've accomplished this, we answer, first of all, that it took a shared vision. Then, hard work and a willingness to dismiss our differences in service to something bigger.

Perhaps the drive to create exists on an unconscious, deeply personal level, a desire to make art in order to connect with others. If this is true, then more than anything, it may be the sweet vibrations of human interactions that inspire new expression.

Lightning Bolts and Meatballs

You wind up creating from silence, like painting a picture on a blank canvas that could bring tears to somebody's eyes. As songwriters, our blank canvas is silence. Then we write a song from an idea that can change somebody's life.

—Rodney Atkins,
"11 Questions With Rodney Atkins," *The Boot*

My husband is a musician, and from time to time we join forces to write songs, me proposing the lyrics, Tom working to set them to music. It's rewarding but challenging, and we have lots of questions—*do these lyrics make sense? Do they go with the melody? What should we do about the chord progression, the bridge?* And always we wonder: *How does this songwriting thing happen anyway?*

For answers we look to our songwriter's group: ten or twelve writers and musicians who gather regularly to talk songwriting and share what we have written. One particularly hot June evening, the conversation went like this:

"Sometimes songwriting is hard work," one person said, "and sometimes it's like channeling," as if a great force is working through you, and you are just the person writing down the words, strumming out the chords.

"There are times you're struck by lightning," another offered, "and you get a great song." "No," a bluesman countered. "For me, it's more like a meatball flying down out of the sky!"

We laugh. Whatever it may be—channeling some spiritual entity, a lightning bolt out of the blue—or a meatball!—it is a comfort sharing our experiences.

As the evening progressed, Ron sang "Old Friends," his song about friends now lost to him; Terry performed "Let's Fly Away" about 9-11 and the passengers on board Flight 93; and Lia, the youngest of the group, sang about "building a house on hallowed ground." She sang a cappella. "I don't have the music yet," she apologized, "and it's not finished," but as she sang, we recognized that what she had written was moving and beautiful, and would go on to become a terrific song.

What a marvelous thing for writers—whether they be songwriters or writers of the written word—to share the wonders of the creative life, as well as the doubts and frustrations that go along with it. And receive a little encouragement to keep going. "I've written a lot of bad songs," one songwriter said, "but the more I keep at it, more and more the good ones come."

Silent Companions

*For me, trees have always been the most penetrating
preachers.*

—Hermann Hesse,
Bäume: Betrachtungen und Gedichte

Creativity is in our bones, hardwired into our operating systems. Jan
Phillips says that creativity is our birthright. It's like an inner switch
that's always there—how we love, stories that spill from our mouths,
new ideas—all coming from within. But sometimes what pops up are
things we can't put into words or form. We don't know how to provide the necessary oxygen, the boost needed to bring the idea to
fruition. Whether it is a sculpture or poem or an interpretive dance, the
challenge is always to find the right image or word, the exact nuance.
We have to find what moves us, and that someone or something arrives
in different forms.

We know when something is right, it clicks into place like a perfectly placed Lego piece. Maybe you're searching for the last image
in a family montage you're creating, and finally, spotting a certain
snapshot, everything gels. Or walking along a trail, you stumble
upon the perfect composition of rock and sky for a photograph. It's
the unexpected note, the unexpected color, the unexpected angle that
provides clarity. How does it happen, this sudden discovery? This
spontaneous fitting into place?

My friend Stan loves whittling and carving wood, finding great
satisfaction, especially, in creating hand-made whistles. He spends
hours selecting the proper branch. His thumb is rough and notched
from scraping his knife over lengths of pine or walnut—carving the
whistle to the right size, the precise shape, cutting the mouthpiece

just at the correct angle. One wall of his basement is covered with a great assortment of different types of whistles—dog whistles, slide whistles, police whistles, and kazoos—many in bright blues and reds. And when he plays them, the sounds produced may be high and tinkly or mellow and low. On his slide whistles, he imitates a falling sound as if he'd hit "Bankrupt" on Wheel of Fortune. Again, we must ask, where does his ingenuity come from?

"God-Given inspiration is what guides me," Stan says. "Think about what a tree dowser does. That's what I do. Finding the right tree, the right branch, to carve." For three generations, his family has owned an apple orchard, and he loves to walk among "his old friends, his silent companions." "It's the tree's life force that calls to me," he says.

"Trees are sanctuaries," Hermann Hesse wrote. "Whoever knows how to speak to them, whoever knows how to listen to them, can learn the truth."[80] We all search for the truth, *our truth*.

When we open ourselves to learning from the world around us, we aren't afraid to open ourselves to other voices, including those in nature. And when we do, the essentials of life become known to us.

For Stan, carving whistles was satisfying, nurturing. It fed his creative bent. But most remarkable about his passion was revealed walking in the apple orchard. It didn't insist or have the need to declare anything, but offered instead a rich empty space of silence, and Stan listened.

---

[80] Herman Hesse, *Wandering: Notes and Sketches* (New York: Farrar, Straus & Giroux, 1972).

Dream-Chasing with Friends

At times our own light goes out and is rekindled by a
spark of another person. Each of us has cause to think
with deep gratitude of those who have lighted the flame
within us.

—Albert Schweitzer,
Out Of My Life and Thought: An Autobiography

Maybe you've noticed that when you're around close friends, good things just happen. It's that way with me. My "sisterhood," a community of six like-minded companions, recently celebrated twenty-five years of friendship, our bond beginning with a backpacking trip to the Rocky Mountains. For the trip, we needed to pack in essentials for six days— our own food and cooking supplies, tent, and sleeping bag—about fifty pounds of dead weight. To ensure we would be up to the task, we trained for several months beforehand: walking, lifting weights, doing whatever we could to increase our endurance. For me, working that hard became a way to create new space for myself. Dropping out of my head into my physical body, I pushed myself far beyond what I ever imagined. By the end of the trip, it seemed that other challenges in my life were less formidable, more doable.

At the time of our first trip, we six were professional women: in business, education, in private therapeutic practice, all of us with a clear sense of who we were and what we wanted to achieve in life. We were, as they say, in the thick mix of climbing the ladder, furthering our education, and raising families. I was trying to write poetry at night after my teenaged girls went to bed, but found myself struggling with a lack of focus and just plain fatigue. But on this trip, an epiphany took place: my women friends helped me change my outlook, and I realized how scribbling words brought me deeper into a world I loved.

When you sleep outside in tents at eleven thousand feet and trace the outlines of Orion and Cassiopeia in the night sky, everything becomes clearer. You see your life telescoped and begin to realize what's really important. This can be both satisfying and terrifying. Certain priorities need to shift. You understand this now: some things *are* more important than others. Listening to my friends talk freely about their challenges and obstacles helped put mine into perspective. They spoke of their glories, their warts, their hopes; and in seeing how courageous they were, how they allowed themselves to be vulnerable, my own stumbling blocks seemed less daunting. I felt hopeful again, heartened. Then a shooting star streaked across the sky, and I knew that, along with my friends, the universe was talking to me that night, encouraging me to keep on with what burned inside, keep on with my dream of writing.

But it's not easy being a dream-chaser. How do you do it? First, take baby steps. Then open your heart, be ready to listen and make some tough decisions. Backpacking is not for sissies, and neither is following your dreams. Put yourself in the company of good friends, and when you need to, ask for help until the firm earth of the world you love is beneath your feet.

A Story, A Story

There is no greater power on earth than story.
—Libba Bray, *The Diviners*

One June not that many years ago, I spent a week camping in West Virginia with my son, daughter-in-law, and three wonderful grandchildren. What a time we had! We camped in the Canaan Valley, one of the highest wetland areas in the United States. There we hiked, took a birdwatching expedition, listened to frogs, and just enjoyed being together in the beautiful world.

What was most memorable about the trip, however, was the storytelling we did. Jessie, my eight-year-old granddaughter, started it, asking me to tell a story about Great-Grandma (my mother who'd recently passed away). "Tell a story about when she was a little girl," Jessie asked. So I told about Great-Grandma stepping on a piece of glass while running around barefoot, and soaking her foot in a washtub to ease it out. That led to other stepping-on-glass-while-going barefoot incidents, my husband's bicycle wreck stories, and other childhood mishaps.

Jakey wanted to hear about camping trips when I was a girl, so I told the camping-trip-that-didn't-happen-because-of-the-flood story, and the story about pitching our tent on a slope and sliding downhill in our sleep. We all told stories, everyone but fourteen-month-old Joshey, who sat wide-eyed on his sleeping bag, taking it all in.

What is there about sitting around the campfire, on the porch, or around the kitchen table listening to someone tell a story? Perhaps it is the delight in the drama, the thrill of a tale; or the wonder in imagining what it would be like to live in another time and another place, putting yourself in the action. Maybe it is the child in us that loves letting the words of another spill over us, enthralling us, and all we have to do is listen.

Sue Monk Kidd said that "stories have to be told or they die, and when they die, we can't remember who we are or why we're here."[81] Leslie Marmon Silko believes that stories are "all we have to fight off illness and death."[82] I think that in listening to stories, we are looking for meaning and connection. We are looking for hope. The bottom line is that we want, need, and thrive on stories. And in whatever medium we create—music, dance, sculpture, painting, or writing novels—we are *always* creating story.

Recently, I ran across a poster which contains this quote by an unknown author: "Live. Create. Tell the story. Repeat." What a magnificent way to be alive!

---

[81] Sue Monk Kidd, *The Secret Life of Bees* (New York: Penguin, 2001).

[82] Leslie Marmon Silko, *Ceremony* (New York: Penguin Books, 1986).

Mentors Make the Difference

A mentor is someone who allows you to see the hope inside yourself.

—Oprah Winfrey,
interview on WCVB-TV 5 News CityLine

Cultivating a mentor relationship may be one of the most important things you do for your creative life. Why is it so important? Mentors are the quintessential wisdom keepers of the art world, acting as caretakers of tradition, passing along historical and cultural knowledge of the craft. A mentor's role is like that of an elder, listening deeply, then conveying the direction and requisite skills so others won't lose their way. Their mission is helping artists grow deeper into their art.

Do you have a mentor? They come to us in all kinds of ways. You may meet them face to face at art shows, writing conferences, or in your local artist community, or they may be artists in your field you court from afar. In some educational and work settings, mentor relationships are established formally with agreed-upon meeting times and expectations. Or, as is often the case in creative mentorships, the mentor relationship is informal, a more experienced artist taking a novice under her wing, recognizing ability and potential and wanting to help it along.

However they come to you and whatever form the mentor-mentee relationship may take, when each invests in the relationship, it can be invaluable—for both parties. While the benefits may seem to accrue primarily to the mentee, mentorship also helps the master. "Keep[ing] your mind young and your skills fresh," according to Marten Mickos, and besides that, providing a link back "to the original you who became so excellent," the creative gift returning full-circle to reenergize and inspire.[83]

During different times in my life, I've had mentors as a new teacher, a young mother, and as a woman going into the next (older) stage of my life. I've also had and continue to derive inspiration from mentors in my writing life who encourage me to go beyond accepting merely "good enough," to strive for excellence. And when I'm in the doldrums—stuck, blocked, lacking in confidence, they provide the lift I need to get me going again.

An artist mentor can help liberate you from un-productive patterns, suggest new pathways into a project, and assist you in recognizing the sparks of originality which you may not be able to see yourself. They have struggled as you have struggled, have despaired and started over. They possess that bit of pizzazz you want to latch on to. Most importantly, they see something in you. They *believe* in you.

Perhaps the most famous mentor-mentee relationship is that of Bohemian-Austrian poet Rainer Maria Rilke and young Franz Xaver Kappus. In his *Letters to a Young Poet*, Rilke declines to criticize Kappus' poetry and instead writes, "I can't give you any advice but this: to go into yourself and see how deep the place is from which your life flows; at its source you will find the answer to the question of whether you must create."[84]

We all need help from time to time. If we are fortunate enough to have a mentor willing to stand with us and show us the way, to open their minds and hearts to us, it is a gift like no other.

---

[83] Marten Mickos, qtd. by Laurence Bradford, "8 Tips For an Amazing Mentor Relationship," *Forbes*, January 31, 2018. https://www.forbes.com/sites/laurencebradford/2018/01/31/8-tips-for-an-amazing-mentor-relationship/#6fd40e6021e2.

[84] Rainer Maria Rilke, *Letters To a Young Poet* (New York: W.W. Norton 1993).17).

Creative Karma

If you send out goodness from yourself, or if you share
that which is happy or good within you, it will all come
back to you multiplied ten thousand times.

—John O'Donohue,
A Book of Celtic Wisdom

From 2005-2009, the TV sitcom *My Name is Earl* featured a slackard good-for-nothing who discovers he holds a $100,000 lottery ticket. He is overjoyed, jubilant. But just as Earl realizes his good fortune, he is struck by a car, then wakes in a hospital bed to find his lottery ticket gone. It is karma, he believes, the forces of the world punishing him for the hurt he has done to others. And from then on, Earl dedicates himself to righting the wrongs he has committed in the past.

I only watched a few episodes but found the idea of some sort of cosmic karma intriguing. "As ye sow, so shall ye reap," the Bible says, suggesting that in the grand scheme of things, we get what's coming to us. We get what we deserve. I'm not sure I believe that. Bad things happen to the innocents of the world, to those who have done only good; and, as we know, right does not always prevail. Injustice is everywhere.

However, I do feel that the good we do comes back to us. We give of ourselves, and in return we receive. Not in a quid pro quo sort of fashion and not in the same measure. But when we contribute to the good of the world, in large part or small, the world becomes a little better, and it eventually makes its way back to us.

My writer friend Gina speaks of the concept of creative karma, that as writers we need to help one another—share news of an upcoming conference, a submission opportunity, or a new way to reach potential readers. We can help in big ways, reading a manuscript and offering constructive, kind feedback; and we can help in smaller ways, providing an encouraging word to someone struggling or blocked creatively.

I am fortunate to live in a community that provides opportunities for writers and artists of all kinds. Several coffeehouses feature open mic nights for musicians to play their music, and for poets and other writers to share what they have written. And what is shared is soulful, from the heart. It is difficult to be an artist, we know that, and so we help one another—with a smile, a thumbs up, a one or five dollar bill in the tip jar. These are small gestures, but to someone experiencing doubt and disappointment, but still trying to make it as an artist, it can mean everything.

When we go out of our way to provide an encouraging word, to say yes to helping each other, we set events in motion. The world shifts a little, becomes a little more kind. "You have been created in order that you might make a difference," Andy Andrews said. "You have within you the power to change the world."[85]

---

[85] Andy Andrews, *The Butterfly Effect: How Your Life Matters* (Nashville: Thomas Nelson; 2010).

For Your Journey

Perhaps it's a matter of time or priority, but many of us struggle between our need for independence and our need for relationship. Do we really need community? According to Margaret Wheatley and Myron Kellner-Rogers, we do. When we choose to live our lives without belonging, "we give up the meaningful life that only can be discovered in a relationship with others."[86] Artists may question the commitment to relationship and community because we may feel it robs us of our uniqueness and takes us away from our precious time. But when we participate in community, we come to realize that the gifts we give and receive benefit us and all the lives involved.

1. Much has been written about the topic of friendship in literature. Consider how these special relationships can serve as models to us: Sherlock Holmes and John Watson in *The Adventures of Sherlock Holmes,* and Huck and Jim in *The Adventures of Huckleberry Finn.* Make a list of exceptional friendships you know about or have observed. Identify what have been the defining characteristics of these relationships. In what ways do the friends support each other? What does it look like to be loyal and trustworthy? How did the relationships enhance the individuals' quality of life or improve their outcomes? Now choose one and write, paint, or sculpt, conveying the unique bonds in the relationship.

2. Consider a long view of your life. *Who were the important teachers, coaches, or mentors in your life? What important roles did they play? How did they help you dream of something*

[86] Margaret Wheatley and Myron Kellner-Rogers, "The Promise and Paradox of Community," *The Community of the Future.* Jossey-Bass, 1998.

different, something bigger? Choose one. Using a variety of visual images or symbols such as photographs, magazine clippings or chosen words, select those that pique your artistic interest and explore the subject of mentoring.

3. Read the poem "Locking Yourself Out, Then Trying to Get Back In" by Raymond Carver. *Think about those times you were locked out from things and make a list of those experiences. How did it feel being locked out? Or that you didn't belong? What were the details of that experience? Who was with you? Where were you? If it happened again, would you do anything differently? Do you still want "in"? Take another perspective, reflect on any time that you were the one that locked someone out. Choose any media that takes you to the heart of rejection and create.*

4. One of our most important relationships is the one we have with ourselves. How do we treat ourselves? With kindness and acceptance? With impatience and anger? Do you become upset with yourself when you do not meet your creative goals? Or believe your talents as an artist do not measure up? Your sense of self impacts your ability to achieve. *Consider for two weeks rating yourself daily on how you feel regarding your creative life. How did you do? Were there any connections with your productivity and your perception of self? If so, what are you going to do about it?*

Chapter Eight:
What It Takes

The Sandhills of the Mind

Inspiration exists, but it has to find us working.
—Pablo Picasso, *Cities Speak*

Every summer I drive through the Nebraska Sandhills—an area of rolling sand dunes and prairie grass loosely rooted in the shifting soil. I love these hills, stark as they often are—especially during dry times—the treelessness, the brown or rust-colored prairie grass, and the frequent "blowouts" where swirling winds erode portions of the hills into empty, sandy bowls. Little rain falls, and it seems a barren plain.

But beneath this apparent desert is the great Ogallala Aquifer, a vast underwater lake of fresh water. It is an incredible resource, in some places the reservoir so close to the surface that water percolates up through the sand to form shallow ponds. Deer, the red fox, geese, and all manner of other wildlife thrive here, and farmers and ranchers need only sink their wells a few feet to hit water.

I love this idea of an underground resource we cannot see, but which is there, nevertheless, so close that we can tap into it with ease and partake in what it has to offer. As creative beings, we all have times of drought, times when the ideas and words do not come. The idea is there, we know—the words we want to write—but we cannot access them. If only we were in a place like the sandhills of the mind, where the reservoir of inspiration is near the surface, where it can easily bubble up into our consciousness, and we can do our best work.

To find inspiration, writer and innovator Mitchell Ditkoff suggests that in many instances, we must first go through a "period of struggle." "It is sustained and focused effort towards a specific goal . . ." he says, "that ultimately prepares the ground for creative insights."[87] We must work hard—stare at the blank canvas, write clunky first drafts, hit our heads up against brick walls. But then we must relax, sleep, take a walk, do what we need to turn the conscious mind off, and let the revelations arrive when they will.

So maybe it's a two-step process: Work hard, then relax. Work harder, relax again. Not very profound, and something most of us do anyway. The working-hard part, at least. We drive through the barren hills, our hands gripping the steering wheel, foot jammed on the accelerator. But sometimes we need to stop and pull off to the side of the road. We need to relax a little, take a bit of a respite. And when we do, we may find ourselves in a place where inspiration bubbles to the surface like water from an underground reservoir. For that great well of thought and ideas *is* there. We need to work hard—then step away from the struggle, and let the insights come.

[87] Mitchell Ditkoff, "Great Moments in Creativity," *Idea Champions*, http://www.ideachampions.com/article_aha.shtml.

The Eye in the Heart

Your own reasons to make are reason enough. Create whatever causes a revolution in your heart.

—Elizabeth Gilbert, *Big Magic*

In a lecture I attended as part of my MFA writing program, Tom Paine, my mentor and short story writer, proposed an approach to writing he called "looking to *the eye in the heart.*"

"You have an eye in the heart," he said. "What you write on the page is an image of who you are," and who you are comes from your heart—what you love and how you love. "Go find your heart," he maintained, "and you will be a better writer." Or musician or visual artist. Whatever type of creativity you choose to pour out the essence of all that you are.

So how do we go about *finding* our hearts? The answer to that, I believe, is very much the way we love. We go through most days with chain link fences around our hearts. We don't allow others in; we don't allow even ourselves in to feel what we are feeling, to acknowledge what we love. But when we create art, we must be unguarded, alive, the doors and windows to our inner selves wide open. That means yearning and desiring, wanting badly, even if that intense wanting could lead to pain. Remember the first time you fell in love? The tug in the stomach, the excitement, how you could be pierced by love? Oh, it could be ecstasy or it could be a world of hurt. We allow ourselves to be vulnerable when we love, and we need that same kind of vulnerability when we write.

In the cartoon strip *Peanuts,* from time to time we see an image of Snoopy sitting atop his doghouse with his typewriter, the caption "It is a dark and stormy night . . ." or "His was a story that had to be told," and in the next frame, "Maybe not." We are all Snoopy at our typewriters, wanting something wonderful to emerge as our fingers strike the keyboard. Sometimes succeeding and sometimes not. In another cartoon, Snoopy again is pecking away at the keys and a thought bubble rises above him. "Writing is hard work." This is true. But also "Writing is *heart* work."[88]

Recently, as I was revising a novel I'd been working on for some time, I discovered that when a particular chapter or scene was limping along, it was usually due to one of two things: 1) "bad" writing or 2) the writing was too much with the head as opposed to the heart. Of course, there are many more ways a piece of writing can go wrong, but these are two biggies for me.

We are often fearful of sentiment, not wanting to be overly syrupy or saccharine. This is a legitimate concern, but I would suggest that if we must err, let us do so on the side of the heart. If we see a piece is overly sentimental, we can always edit. But let us first write with the emotions, let us write from our hearts.

---

[88] Charles Schulz, "It Was a Dark and Stormy Night, Snoopy" (New York: Ballantine Books, 2004).

The Dailyness of Creativity

Dripping water hollows out stone, not through force but with persistence.

—Ovid, *Letters From the Black Sea*

How do we go about accomplishing the creative goals we have, living up to the seeds of possibility within? We all have dreams and goals. Maybe it's a novel to be written, a story that needs to be told. It might be a dream of painting a series of still lifes based on the work of Cezanne. But when the blank canvas or computer screen presents itself before us, the task seems insurmountable. How do we overcome fear and inertia—that sense of being overwhelmed in order to allow the process to begin?

Perhaps the biggest obstacle arises out of fear that we are not worthy. We work up too much anxiety about the creative act, thinking that to paint well, we must be painters extraordinaire, so that every time we stand before our easels, what emerges with each brushstroke must be brilliant, profound, Carnegie Prizewinning potential. Of course, that is not so. "Don't think about making art, just get it done," Andy Warhol said. "Let everyone else decide if it's good or bad, whether they love it or hate it. While they are deciding, make even more art."[89]

We believe that the best way to overcome the fear involved with creating art is to remove its mystique, to consider it in all its "dailyness." If we are dancers or sculptors, every day we practice our routines, chip away a little stone. No big deal. Sometimes we dance and sculpt well, sometimes not so well; but as much as possible, we

---

[89] Andy Warhol, *The Philosophy of Andy Warhol (From A To B & Back Again)* (San Diego: Harcourt Brace Jovanovich, 1975).

work daily. What about the other work we do? Every morning we rise and take care of our families. They are important to us, and we do what we can to nurture them and provide for their needs. We do it because we must, without thinking twice about it. Our creative projects—the novels and poems, the paintings within us—are important, too, and we need to nurture them as well. Regularly, as a matter of habit. The dailyness of creativity doesn't mean you have to write five pages of your novel every day, or complete a sketch of your next painting. It means spending whatever time you can. Novels are written chapter by chapter, scene by scene; and musical scores, note by note. One step after another after another. *Slow and steady*, the old saying goes, *easy does it*. We all know these old maxims. So it is with creativity. Easy does it.

And if we don't write or paint every day? If day after day goes by, or week after week, and we find that we are not working? Well, then, we forgive ourselves. We are human beings; life happens, and procrastination happens too. We forgive ourselves and start again. We keep working, keep on the path to our dreams and goals, and as we do, we draw closer and closer to realizing them.

Doing Everything We Can

Composition seems to be impossible with a head full of joints of mutton & doses of rhubarbs.

—Jane Austen, *Letter to Cassandra Austen*

Psychologist and philosopher William James studied the "habits of order" and recommended that "the more of the details of our daily lives we can hand over [to established habit] . . . the more our higher powers of mind will be set free for their own proper work."[90] When we follow routines, we put ourselves on autopilot and are able to concentrate on the mental or creative activity we desire. We are free to seize inspiration when it comes. But what habits? You have to decide what works best for you. What routines would you choose?

For me, it's easy enough to promise myself I'll get up early every morning and write. There's a certain romance to this idea—living a life committed to rising in the wee hours to work on an essay or poem. But at six-thirty in the morning, the sun stalks the dark sky, sneaking up behind the old cottonwoods like a slow spotlight shining on them. First the tree trunks clothed in white-pink, then the lower branches until the tree is on fire, the view so extravagant I can't concentrate on anything else. Then, too, the sluggish systems of my body haven't awakened yet; I'm still chugging along in low gear. I need coffee, and I need time for my brain to come alive. Mid-morning, however, my creative juices begin to flow, so I schedule that time of the day to work.

Over the last decade, social psychologists have learned a great deal about the science of willpower. They've found that in order to

---

[90] William James, *Principles of Psychology*: *Volume 1* (New York: Henry Holt & Co., 1918) 122.

stick with our resolutions and meet our creative goals, we must be sure that they are *realistic, attainable,* and *"right"* for us. In addition, it helps to start small. Willpower has limitations. So, if we zero in on the two or three goals we consider most important, our likelihood of achieving them will increase. With success on these initial goals, we'll gain confidence, making the remaining goals less challenging.

Lastly, our ability to reduce mental distractions and focus is vital. It's human nature to daydream, plan grocery lists, ruminate about all sorts of things. And while a certain amount of daydreaming is needed for the creative process, there are times we must buckle down and concentrate on the project before us.

How do we get back on track? Three things have helped me. First, I find a quiet place to write, usually my favorite yellow chair. Sometimes, I stare out my window and watch birds swoop, or doodle on my legal pad. Second, exercise. This might mean taking my dog for a quick walk or doing a few yoga poses. Third, if my mind is still wandering, I practice centering and deep-breathing meditations. Finally, if these don't help me focus, I bring out my crystals. I'll do everything I can to make my dreams real.

When We Believe

You have to believe. Otherwise, it will never happen.
—Neil Gaiman, *Stardust*

Since the first time we realized our hands could be tools, women have worked with clay, woven textiles, arranged stones into pleasing patterns, designed jewelry, and fashioned all kinds of amazing art. This, in addition to oftentimes back-breaking work to provide for their families. They made things beautiful because they couldn't help themselves, because the desire to create was one of the truest things in their hearts. Such is the case with generations of women in my family, managing in spite of hardship and family and work obligations to find their voices through creative expression. How did they do it? They kept going—working constantly, remaining steady. Believing in the midst of difficulties, there was something more.

Grandma K managed two farms, sold eggs weekly at the corner grocery store, canned fifty quarts of tomatoes and green beans every fall, taught Sunday School, and raised three children. Somehow, she found time to become a hat maker, crafting beautiful felt and woolen hats decorated with feathers and wooden buttons. And to paint— delicate patterns of roses on saucers and cups, intertwining leaves and vines on serving dishes. During the spring, my other grandmother, Grandmother M, drove a team of horses, Joe and Molly, to plant corn and wheat; and in the fall she cured and dried pork for the long winter. It was *hard on hands*, she used to say, *all the salt*. But late at night she turned her attention to something she loved—planning designs and putting them to paper, then cutting up worn dishtowels, overalls and blankets to make quilts.

The Fire Inside

Early in my life, my mother added to her duties as a farm wife to take on employment as a bookkeeper. At dawn three mornings a week, I'd wake to the frantic sounds of chickens clucking, then a resounding whack; and before she went to work, Mom had two or three birds cleaned and soaking in brine. And on weekends during haying season, she prepared big meals for the hired help. Yet somehow, she squeezed out a few moments here and there to paint: landscapes of old barns, flowers, or whimsical oils of children.

My two daughters laughingly say it requires "moving mountains" to make room for creativity, but they do so on a regular basis. To satisfy her interest in creative design, Allison combines bright colors, varying textures and different art forms to accent her home. To "get into her bones," she dances hip-hop whenever she can. Monica, besides nurturing a garden of heirloom plants, loves to write. Recently she created and presented a monologue at the "Listen to Your Mother" performance series in her hometown.

Sometimes finding spare time for your creative life can be like finding rivers in a desert, like making something from nothing. Difficult, but not impossible. We are all after the same thing—uncovering the deep, sweet marrow of our lives. And when we are determined, when we believe that creativity is as important as oxygen, there *is* enough time. Each of us has a lion's heart. Believe, and somehow, we will find the way.

The Power of the Deadline

A hammer made of deadlines is the surest tool for crushing writer's block.

—Ryan Lilly, *Write Like No One Is Reading*

As much as I love a clean and tidy house—everything spick and span, the clutter picked up and put away—the feel of a vacuum cleaner in my hand, a dishcloth, or a mop makes me crazy. But there is nothing that will make me spring into action like company coming. Then I am on a mission, cleaning and organizing, and when it's all done, I'm tired but happy, ready to enjoy the pleasure of having company. I even enjoy the time *after* my visitors leave, basking in the delight of living in such well-kept surroundings. So, why do I put off these types of chores until absolutely necessary?

It's human nature to procrastinate, to put off until tomorrow what we should be doing today. Even when procrastination brings about more discomfort than it would just taking a deep breath and starting in on what we've been avoiding. Does this ring a bell at all? Procrastination to some degree is familiar territory for all of us, and most especially for artists and writers.

This is where the power of the deadline comes in. We writers want to wait for inspiration, but while inspiration may fail us, there is nothing like a deadline to get us writing. "A deadline gets a writer's work done better and faster than any inspiration," A.A. Patawaran says, "if only because inspirations don't always come, but the deadline is always there."[91]

We first encounter deadlines in school—where book reports and

---

[91] A.A. Patawaran, *Write Here Write Now: Standing at Attention Before My Imaginary Style Dictator* (Mandaluyong: Anvil Publishing, 2016).

essays are due on a regular basis. Some of us work towards our due dates a little each day, slowly but surely making progress towards the completion of the assignment. Others love to wait until the last minute—starting late, working feverishly, and finishing the task in the nick of time. Whichever method you choose, the deadline motivates us and leads to accomplishment.

But what if we don't have a teacher spurring us on with a due date? An editor or publisher pushing us with a deadline? Many of us are our own taskmasters. We set our own deadlines (or not) and determine the consequences if we fail to perform. We are not writers unless we write, so how do we keep on keeping on?

When setting your own deadlines, it helps to have someone to keep you accountable. Writing with a writing partner (as in completing this book—with certain essays to be written within a one or two week period) helped to keep us working steadily. Some writing friends like to pledge to two or three of their peers that they will have forty pages of their novel written by the next time the friend group meets—or to have made a certain number of poetry submissions. Each individual is responsible for setting his or her goal, and the responsibility to "report in" helps provide the sense of urgency and the motivation to keep working. Deadlines keep us energized, keep us on the road to achieving our goals. We do what we can to invoke their power.

Staying in the Game

You may not control life's circumstances, but getting to be the author of your life means getting to control what you do with them.

—Atul Gawande,
Being Mortal: Medicine and What Matters in the End

Sometimes we hit walls, real ones, such as those life-altering physical ailments that keep us from our art, from doing what we love. We may be dealing with the aftermath of illness or injury, pain and weakness that relegate creativity to second place, or third. In some instances, we may abandon the life of the imagination altogether. Yet, if we *will* our art to re-emerge, to take some form, we become invigorated, connected again to our most authentic selves. Persevering helps us find that spark. Ask yourself: "How can I keep doing what I love? What can I do to get rolling again in spite of the aches and pains that are part of what I now call me?"

Chuck Maranzano, a musician who plays the saxophone, clarinet, and flute in several bands, says that while his tunes may serve to provide a balm in the lives of others, the music has in fact saved his *own* life. He suffers from arthritis in his fingers, shoulders, and knees, but it is in playing music he is able to keep going. He attests that he just "blows through the pain," so he can get to that special place where his life is enriched, where he finds meaning.

There may be times, however, when gritting your teeth and keeping on in spite of pain and difficulty may not be enough. But if you are willing to modify, change your routines, and dig deeper, you can still live out your creativity. After Jeremy, a gifted visual artist, experienced a traumatic brain injury in high school, he continued painting, exploring different art styles. He found that while his earlier pieces featured a great deal of detail work, his style post-injury became more abstract and fluid. He adjusted, and after his high school graduation, went on to complete an MFA in Art.

Our bodies talk to us, and we have to listen. Physical changes and challenges must be recognized, but how much do we let them affect our creative spirits? I remember how excited I was to receive an invitation to share my poems at my first open mic appearance. Yet I almost turned it down because I was recovering from an extended hospital stay and didn't see myself as strong enough. To live a creative life, we must learn how to experience the best of what we know, push through physical obstacles, and move closer to the heat of our passion. Turning that fierceness and confidence into action helps to keep in our lives that which enlivens and fulfills.

Make your life count. Keeping on can become an antidote to ennui and everyday challenges. Your art can be a change-maker, engaging with the world in the wonderful ways you know how. Trust what it brings as one of your very reasons for being. You don't have control over many things, and life doesn't give you immunity from difficulties, but making creativity a part of yours is a *choice*. Make it yours.

Animal Power

*I sometimes look into the face of my dog Stan and see
a wistful sadness and existential angst, when all he is
actually doing is slowly scanning the ceiling for flies.*

—Merrill Markoe, *What the Dogs Have Taught Me:
And Other Amazing Things I've Learned*

All our lives we've heard that dogs are man's best friend, praised for their undying devotion and loyalty, the way they listen carefully to whatever we say. As I've watched my four-legged friend so engaged with everything around him, I've often wondered if seeing the world through his eyes could nudge me to greater awareness, give me a new perspective—perhaps even improve my creative life. Author and dog admirer Tony Williams in "The Writer Walking the Dog: Creative Writing Practice and Everyday Life" believes so.

Williams found that dog-walking may be beneficial to fostering imagination and curiosity in that it provides a "break in creative consciousness."[92] Isn't that what happens when we shift in our thinking? Consider alternative realities? By thinking about something other than the project at hand, Williams theorizes, creative thoughts can emerge. He also finds that dog-walking provides writers the "time to mull over" their written work[93], allowing an opportunity for the novelist to reflect, for example, on questions about plot and tone: *does it make sense for the protagonist to be an only child? Should she be so angry?*

In my life, walking Cooper, our eight-year-old yellow lab, gives

[92] Tony Williams, "The Writer Walking the Dog: Creative Writing Practice and Everyday Life," *American, British, and Canadian Studies* 20, no. 1 (2012): 231.
[93] Ibid, 233.

me a break from writing and revision. The movement works to free up my mind. The walks—involving lots of sniffing (on Cooper's part) as well as frequent stops to inspect interesting shrubs—follow a nature path overgrown with tangled vegetation and aging ash trees. One morning, I decided to adjust my vision to Cooper's height to see what lay ahead. We walked a little way when suddenly he stopped, and I came nose-to-nose with a tree's outreaching lower branches, took in the leaves' intricate patterns, smelled the musty odor of damp earth.

There's something to say about up-close encounters with the world. You see differently, almost as if you've forgotten you have eyes and ears. Your senses are heightened so you're able to see more: whorled leaf patterns, the elbow-knobs on branches. You feel more intensely, sometimes forming intimate relationships with those things around you. My walk from Cooper's viewpoint left me marveling at the depth and detail, the significance of the things of this world, as well as that of my world before: evoking a childhood memory of a cellar that smelled of old and rotting things, spiders skittering into corners.

Think about the animal power you have. Flex your muscles. Sniff around. The natural world can open you to throbbing domains—introduce you to worlds of color, shape, and scent, and cultivate in you a longing to re-connect to memories of the past. You will become freer. You can move outside the straitened confines you may have outlined for your life. Walk your dog or your neighbor's dog, and experience things you never expected: noisy crows flying overhead like those in Van Gogh's painting, walnut shells surprising you like hiccups rolling on the ground.

Two Types of Creativity

Writing is like riding a bike. Once you gain momentum, the hills are easier. Editing, however, requires a motor and some horsepower.

—Gina McKnight, *The Blackberry Patch*

The British-American film *Genius* revolves around the relationship between writer Thomas Wolfe and his editor, Max Perkins. In the opening scene, a rumpled, wild-haired Wolfe enters Perkins' office carrying a foot-high stack of dirty, dog-eared paper. It is what he considers to be his masterpiece, the manuscript of his first novel. He gives it to Perkins and pleads with him to read it and consider it for publication.

Perkins agrees, and finds the story to be moving, the writing brilliant, the style sweeping and grand. But it was too much: grandiose at times, dense, the unrelenting prose (brilliant as it was) making it difficult to follow the story. And it was entirely too long. The two agreed to work together, and under Perkins' guidance, the editing process began—crossing out entire sections, simplifying and clarifying, but doing so without losing the magnificence of the original draft. And in 1929, after cutting sixty thousand words, *Look Homeward, Angel* was published to great acclaim. Two types of creativity were involved in bringing this novel to life—the first messy and free-wheeling as Wolfe wrote the first draft, and the second more orderly—shaping and refining.

According to Greek legend, the god Zeus had two sons: Apollo who was the god of logic and reason; and Dionysius, the god of wine and intoxication, chaos and unbridled freedom. Two distinct god-sons, their essential natures diametrically opposite. Using these opposing sets of characteristics, the philosopher Nietsche defined two types of "creative energies." The first type welcomes ideas of the unconscious mind. It is ecstatic, unstructured, sometimes wild; and this he termed Dionysian creativity. The second, Apollonian creativity, is based on harmony and logical thought, and involves aligning artistic elements to create symmetry and beauty. With Dionysian creativity the work comes freely, but it often comes in a mess; and in Apollonian creativity, order is imposed.

We believe that all of us—as people and as artists—use both types of creativity, though we often possess a greater aptitude for one type over the other. Maybe you revel working in great paroxysms of the imagination—crumpled papers and notecards scattered all over, paints and paintbrushes and sketchbooks in disarray, as you work madly to capture a particular image. Or perhaps you can take only so much disorganization before you need to stop and impose some measure of order. Whatever your natural inclination, honor it—the wild Dionysian side of you, or its more orderly brother. Honor it, but recognize that it will take both types of energies to create your art.

Winter Morning Walks

It's the marriage of the soul with nature that makes the intellect fruitful and gives birth to imagination.

—Henry David Thoreau,
The Journal of Henry David Thoreau

In the year 2000, poet Ted Kooser gave a reading at a local public library I will never forget. He had just published a new collection of poems, and began the reading by explaining how the book came into being. Two years previously, he had been diagnosed with cancer, had undergone surgery and radiation therapy, and at that point was just starting the road to recovery. He was weak, and as he writes in the preface to the book, "feeling miserably sorry" for himself. Walking had always been a part of his life, but since his oncologist told him that he must avoid sunlight for a year due to the radiation and resultant skin sensitivity, he put in his two miles every day before dawn.

So he walked, taking the country roads near his home, and gradually he found himself feeling better. During his illness, he had not been writing. But one November day he "surprised" himself at the end of his walk by writing a poem. His walking and writing continued, and he began pasting the poems on postcards and mailing them to his friend and fellow writer, Jim Harrison.

One hundred of those postcard poems make up the book, and oh, what poems they are! Each piece is titled with the date of his walk followed by a brief weather report, then the magic of the poem. For instance, November 15 is "cold and clear," and flying overhead "an anthem of geese." On the morning of January 23rd, it is "twenty-two degrees and very still," and the "road like a levee two hours before dawn . . ."[94]

Poem after brilliant poem follows, short poems, but each with a nugget of surprise that delights, creates a lasting image in the mind, and leaves you thinking in new ways about the world. The book is titled *Winter Morning Walks: One Hundred Postcards to Jim Harrison*, and it is excellent.

Over the years I have thought a great deal about this book, not only in admiration of the poems, but thinking how the book was created. Ted Kooser didn't start on his morning walks with the goal of writing a new book. But with the dailyness of his routine, his decision to follow up his walks by writing, and with (I believe) the magic and the healing power of nature, a memorable book came into being.

---

[94] Ted Kooser, *Winter Morning Walks: One Hundred Postcards to Jim Harrison* (Pittsburgh: Carnegie Mellon University Press, 2000).

For Your Journey

When you choose to become a serious artist, you are in it for the long haul. You cannot learn to dance overnight, or reach proficiency as a musician or writer in six months or a year—or even in a few years. Malcolm Gladwell writes that it takes ten thousand hours of practicing your art before mastery is achieved. You may write three or four "practice" novels, paint hundreds of paintings before you reach that point. How do you keep on? We would suggest that besides persistence, it takes love. Love of your work, the small everyday steps of it, love of the process. Here are some additional suggestions:

1. An important part of keeping on in the creative life is learning to wait. For the idea to come, the solution to the artistic problem. You will have periods of dormancy and times you need to rest. In bicycle riding, you pedal and pedal, working your muscles hard. But now and then it is good and necessary to slow down, coast, and let your muscles recover. While you do, take in the scenery around you: the pristine blue of the sky—or the gray wool blanket of sky—the hills and grasses. *Consider ways to spend some coasting time, some times of idling when your conscious creative mind can rest. Take long walks, putter in the garage, delight in that bicycle ride. What else would you do?*

2. "Motivation is what gets you started," Olympic runner and writer, Jim Ryun said. "Habit is what keeps you going."[95] Not only does habit keep you at your creative projects, it allows "muscle memory" to kick in, so that at six or nine or eleven

---

[95] Jim Ryun, qtd. by Cordner Nelson, *The Jim Ryun Story* (Mountain View, CA: Tafnews Press, 1967).

o'clock when you go to the piano or the pottery studio, your actual work begins quickly—your mind and body settling easily into the groove of work. *Do you have a routine for your work? If not, set a schedule for your creative time. Before you begin, establish a routine. Turn off your phone, put on your painting shirt, and grab a cup of coffee or tea. The familiar feel of your shirt and a sip from your cup will signal to you that it is time to paint or to make music. Create your own set of habits and let them work for you.*

3. In a project that will take a long time, it is important to celebrate milestones, big and small. *When you've completed a series of photographs or made it to the end of a difficult chapter, celebrate with dinner out. At the end of the first draft of your novel, throw a party. Hang up balloons and set flowers and candles burning all over your house. Buy strawberries and chocolate, baguettes and cheese. Then have a few friends over to drink a little bubbly and celebrate with you.*

4. C. G. Jung in *The Archetypes and the Collective Unconscious* explores how many of us—influenced by personal life events and the culture in which we live—begin over time to identify with certain archetypes. Some archetypical models are *wise woman, warrior, bear, lover, hero.* The archetype we identify with impacts how we express ourselves, including how we approach and express our art. You may not fit these given models. *But think you. What animal or entity expresses you? An earthworm? A tiger? What archetype symbolizes your approach to art? Does this awareness help you understand what it takes for you to be an artist? Does it help you find inspiration, establish work priorities and deadlines, persist in spite of challenges? In what ways might your archetype model hold you back?*

Chapter Nine:
Overcoming/Letting Go

Yes, You *Are* Creative

The desire to create is one of the deepest yearnings of the human soul.

—Dieter Uchtdorf, *"Happiness, Your Heritage"*

You may have heard people say, "Oh, I'm not very creative" or "I was born without the creativity gene." Hearing that, you might wonder if you yourself have the inherent "something" it takes to be an original, for the imagination to thrive. And if your latest creative effort falls flat (as it will from time to time) or the bluebirds of creativity haven't flown over your head lately, you may question yourself even further. I know I have. Do I really have within me what it takes to be a writer? To bring forth original and worthy work?

To all who have worried about this, there is good news. Milton Glaser, celebrated graphic designer, said that "there is no such thing as a creative *type*."[96] Dr. Phil Samuel and Dr. Michael Ohler write that "creativity is not a special gift endowed only upon a lucky few. It is for everyone and it is everywhere."[97] Our inherent abilities are greater

---

[96] Milton Glaser, qtd. by Jonah Lehrer, *Imagine: How Creativity Works* (Edinburgh: Canongate, 2012).

[97] Phil Samuel and Michael Ohler, "How Manufacturing Managers Can Tap into the Unlimited Creative Potential of Their Employees," *Industry Week*, October 4, 2012, https://www.industryweek.com/innovation/article/21958563/how-manufacturing-managers-can-tap-into-the-unlimited-creative-poten-

than we would ever imagine. So, let us accept this as a truism—that we are all born with the potential for creativity. The trick is in mining it, bringing it out of the dark, and shining a light on it. First, let us remember that we needn't be an artist in the traditional sense to be considered creative. Creativity can take the form of planning an evening meal or finding the right words to say to a troubled friend. Planning what you will wear for the day or coming up with a way to fix a sagging gate. Okay. But maybe what you *really* want is to paint landscapes that will take your breath away. Write a short story that will make you laugh and cry, and realize something new about what it means to be human in this world.

To enhance creativity, perhaps the best thing we can do is to learn the art of letting go. This means being willing to create badly, put forth mediocre work. Because we must let go of a lot of the "not so good" before the truly fine appears. Let me repeat that. We must let go of the "not so good" before the *truly fine* appears.

It also means shutting off the critics—both your outer critics, anyone who questions your abilities or puts you down—as well as shutting off the *inner* critic. That little voice inside which tells you that what you're doing is foolish, that you're wasting your time. Let those critics go. It means not taking yourself too seriously, being willing to fool around and see what happens. Brene Brown said that "Creativity is the way I share my soul with the world."[98] Creative work is soul work. So give in to your yearnings, let go, and share the spirit that is you. Because, yes, you *are* creative.

---

tial-of-their-employees.

[98] Brene Brown, Interview by Elizabeth Gilbert, "The Way I Share My Soul with the World," *Magic Lessons with Elizabeth Gilbert,* September 30, 2015).

Writing About "Bad" Passions

Make me chaste, Lord, but not quite yet.

—Saint Augustine, *Confessions*

Willa Cather said, "Most of the basic material a writer works with is acquired before age fifteen."[99] Then I shouldn't have been surprised when, leafing through my mother's memory album, I found a startling letter written to my parents many years ago, when I was a teenager. The carefully penned note was from Charlie, a seventy-year old neighbor, who used to help our family doing odd jobs around the farm—mowing, weeding the garden, and tending to us three kids when our parents were busy.

Charlie's letter was newsy and long. He asked about farm prices, who lived on the old place, and how "the kids" were doing. He said nice things about my brother and sister, but of me, he wrote, "She's a very determined little girl. You can't change her mind." Reading his words surprised me a great deal, even hurt a bit, despite the fact that I'd often heard my parents describe me as "stubborn." I thought I'd reserved that aspect of my temperament for my family alone to witness.

I didn't truly resolve Charlie's and my parents' shared opinion of me until I stumbled upon "Microscopic Truthfulness" in Brenda Ueland's *If You Want to Write*. Ueland said that people who write "should not ignore any more the bad passions in themselves . . . but begin to take a good and interested look at these passions and try to understand them."[100] She believed that writers who express

---

[99] Willa Cather, *Willa Cather On Writing* (Lincoln: University of Nebraska Press, 1988).

[100] Brenda Ueland, *If You Want To Write* (Minneapolis: Graywolf Press, 1997).

all the things they think and feel delve deeper, feel more, and write better. We become kinder to ourselves by inviting in the gift of self-compassion and acceptance for all the multiplicities we are. Once we can recognize and honor these passions, no matter what they are, Ueland argues, we learn to respect them, letting them do their work, eventually uncovering a path to happiness.

Haven't we all felt jealous when the poem we submitted to the contest isn't chosen? Or when a friend's short story is accepted for the anthology but not ours—when deep down we feel that ours is just as good? Why do "they" seem to get all the breaks? There *are* inequities in life, times we are treated unfairly, and we can't help but experience jealousy, anger, and perhaps even moments of intense dislike towards our rivals and perceived enemies. These are feelings we usually keep to ourselves.

But expressing our strong passions lets us inhabit tensions that are in our bodies, so that eventually we can release them into the art we create. We become more honest with ourselves, and we crack open, not only to our inner feelings, but to the universal struggles of humankind, accepting certain realities in life, fighting for justice, finding love. When we write these strong feelings into our poems and stories, our characters come alive and speak their truth. We do our most powerful writing, and in the process, we, too, may find solace. Since childhood, I have ached, knowing of the huge disappointments in my father's hard life—his crops ruined by hail, a brother favored in the family business. Writing of the world's injustices has helped me to come to terms with that.

Society expects writers to be thoughtful, expansive thinkers, and agents of change. I acknowledge that and strive toward that ideal. So rather than referring to my stubbornness as one of my "bad" passions, I've learned to reframe it instead as the desired quality of persistence.

With that mental shift, I feel better about my writing and I'm happier, owning it for what it is.

Let Go of Your Little Will

Your little will can't do anything. It takes Great Determination. Great Determination doesn't mean just you making an effort. It means the whole universe is behind you and with you—the birds, trees, sky, moon, and ten directions.

—Katagiri Roshi, qtd. in *Finding Eagle, A Journey Into Modern Day Shamanism* by Marge Hulburt

For a long time now, no one has asked me to put my strong will aside. But Natalie Goldberg in *The True Secret of Writing* does just that. She suggests that when we let go of our little will, it eases open a window for something larger to come through. We want to be inspired, to write a short story that will knock your socks off, a novel that speaks to the passion and yearning and despair and unbounded happiness that is part of the human condition. But how do we do that? While determination and effort are important in motivating us to pick up our pens, the force of will doesn't necessarily get us anywhere. "Better to come to the page with the clouds and sun carrying us," Goldberg says, "the ache in our shoulder, last night's bad sleep, the bills unpaid, and the memory of our son's whistle."[101]

The trick at the beginning of any creative undertaking is to *let go*. Don't overthink or intellectualize, just jump in applying the full strength of your remarkable and impassioned life. Live everything and let the ideas come. Maybe you have a great voice and flirted briefly with the idea of becoming a country and western singer. Write about that. Or perhaps you love sailing and fantasize about traveling

[101] Natalie Goldberg, *The True Secret of Writing* (New York: Atria Books, 2013).

to exotic ports around the world. Start with that and see where the writing takes you.

When you allow yourself to let go, it will lead you to intriguing plots and deeper, more exciting explorations of your characters. Perhaps you will find the mojo to write the story you haven't yet been able to tell. Like my young cousin who wrote about the interior of her car catching fire from an untended cigarette, and her attempts to convince the police officer not to ticket her. When we begin from a bigger place and let the life we imagine as well as the life we experience (or the experiences of others) inform and guide us, we create with more vitality, more color and verve.

Remember the you who was a dreamer, an idealist, who wanted to take the world in your hands and squeeze it for all its juice (maybe that's still you!), the you who stood up to a bully, stood up for what was right. Imagine the you who might have been if you'd been born in a different country, a different century, to different parents.

Start with your great imagination. Find the free-wheeling, hat-tossing part of you, the part that digs deep and flies high. Let go, and as Roshi suggests, the "birds, trees, sky, moon, and ten directions" will get behind you.[102] With this kind of help, you can do almost anything.

---

[102] Katagiri Roshi, qtd. by Marge Hulburt, *Finding Eagle, A Journey Into Modern Day Shamanism* (Missoula: Gone Writing, 2010).

The Gremlin House

I have written eleven books, but each time I think, 'Uh oh, they're going to find me out now. I've run a game on everybody and they're going to find me out.'

—Maya Angelou, *BBC Magazine*

For years I've taken a writing getaway to a cabin along a little stream, and have become familiar with its bends and eddies, each tree along its banks. But one year, there was something new. Across the stream, a willow had lost one of its twin trunks, and someone had used odds and ends and a lot of imagination to transform the stump into a little "house" with a peaked roof. To me, it looked like Winnie the Pooh's house plucked out of the Five Hundred Acre Wood, but a red-lettered sign on the door identified it as the residence of "The Gremlins."

I think of gremlins as mischievous little creatures who throw wrenches into the works of our good intentions. Small beings out to create trouble just as things are going well. Saboteurs. And here they were twenty feet away as I tried to jot down on paper something halfway intelligent.

But the stump house was charming, an enchanting little abode, and I chose to think of its residents as beings of good will, on my side in the creativity business. It had a picket fence and glass jewels by the doorway, and in the attic a door leading out to a balcony. This was a place of the imagination, a place of delight. If there were troublemakers, saboteurs anywhere, they lived in my own head in the form of fear and self-doubt.

We all have experienced this, feeling that we're not good enough, that somehow we're not "real" artists, but impostors. Yet when we excessively self-judge and doubt our abilities, we limit our creativity

189

and potential. So, why do we let self-doubt creep in? It's a way of protecting ourselves from the fear that we won't live up to our expectations. To ward off the terrible feeling that we aren't made of the right "stuff" to be creative.

Doubt is like an itch that won't go away, a toothache impossible to ignore. We start believing there's a limit to creativity and we drew the short stick. That the plain meat and potatoes in front of us is better than any possible feast of tomorrow. We're like the blind man who stays inside his house because he doesn't trust his cane, his teachers, or his personal instincts. He's trapped and so is the artist who allows doubt to imprison him.

How does doubt take hold? It sets in when we hope for a specific outcome for our writing, photograph, or clay pot, but are fearful that our finished creation won't match the image we have in mind—the writing awkward, the color wrong, the shape. The effect is not exactly as we wanted. There's a sense of anxiousness, and we begin to believe we aren't sufficiently creative, or worse, we don't have what it takes to be a real artist.

What can you do to break the chains of doubt? Get those gremlins under control? You can learn to trust yourself. "That which you think," Richard Matheson said, "becomes your world."[103] Feel good about your persistence and the love you have for your work rather than focusing on the end result. Know that you as an artist are a work in progress, learning, growing, becoming better, sometimes taking small steps back, but inevitably moving ahead to more fully inhabit your creativity. When you succeed, when you've done a small thing well, relish that. Know that another small moment will follow, and another and another. We live our best selves into being with action.

---

[103] Richard Matheson qtd. by Albert J. Parisi, "New Jersey Q & A: Richard Matheson; An Influential Writer Returns to Fantasy," *The New York Times*, April 10, 1994.

Slay Your Dragons

Perhaps all the dragons in our lives are princesses who are only waiting to see us act, just once with beauty and courage.

—Rainer Marie Rilke, *Letters To A Young Poet*

In a line from the movie *Out of Africa*, old mapmakers warned that beyond the edge of the world there were dragons—dreadful, horrible to look upon, and out to get us. Luckily, most of the "dragons" we face are in our minds. Still, they loom terribly real above us, and if we are artists, they threaten to undermine our creative spirits.

Dragons appear in the form of self-doubt, procrastination, perfectionism, distraction, ego, and fear. They also come in the form of resistance and attempt to keep us from what we love, from fulfilling our higher selves. Steven Pressfield describes resistance as a force which is powerful and universal, something that plays for keeps and tries to take advantage at every corner.

In what form does resistance appear? Sometimes, unsure of the next step to take in our art, or unable to come up with a fresh idea, we find ourselves doing unnecessary tasks to distract ourselves from getting to work. Cleaning, cleaning, cleaning. Doing the bills. Or it may be a reluctance to try something new. A friend taking a tap dance class wanted me to join in, but I found myself apprehensive. I could still do the shuffle-ball-step—why the angst? Was my ego in the way? Worried I couldn't keep up?

A novelist friend Julie tells the story of her resistance to writing a sex scene, even one that was fairly mild and tastefully written. "I resisted, but something seemed wrong," she said, "the novel, stilted, untrue to its characters." When she realized she was fearful of being judged, she put her fear aside, wrote the scene, and the story came alive.

Now and then we may be resistant to sharing our work or submitting it for publication. Sometimes this is a good thing: refusing to open to public scrutiny work that isn't ready, or publishing a poem which may damage a relationship. Most of the time, however, resistance is born out of feelings of vulnerability and a lack of self-confidence. And if we can overcome it, we will take a step forward in our art.

Since childhood, Jeanne loved to make necklaces of gemstones and Tibetan beads which she gave away as gifts to friends. These were exquisite pieces, dazzling and unique, but when asked why she didn't sell them at local outlets and art fairs, she said they were "too ordinary," and that "no one would buy them." She was resistant. Then good fortune intervened when a dealer spotted her work, and her jewelry business took off.

How do we fight resistance? Stay primitive, Pressfield urges, and let the unconscious mind do her work. Don't overthink, don't overplan, forget the linear mind. Focus on process, not product. Figure out your idea and bring it to the surface by doing the two-step process: action, then reflection. Or, reframe the role of your fears, as Rainer Maria Rilke suggested, thinking of dragons as princesses wanting to see you acting with "beauty and courage."[104]

Resistance is powerful, but not as powerful as your love for your art. Align yourself with this passion and *then* go into battle against the dragon. "We must do our work for its own sake, not for fortune or attention or applause," Pressfield reminds us.[105] When we cultivate heat and enthusiasm, we develop an intense love affair with our creativity. Then we can let ardor be the force that overcomes our resistance.

---

[104] Rainer Maria Rilke, *Letters to a Young Poet*, (New York: W.W. Norton 1993).
[105] Steven Pressfield, *The War of Art: Break Through the Blocks & Win Your Inner Creative Battles* (Black Irish Entertainment, 2002).

Letting Off a Little Steam

The country is so wounded, bleeding, and hurt right now . . . How are we going to heal? Art is the healing force.

—Robert Redford,
National Arts Policy Roundtable 2012

Want to hear some good news for a change? After taking into account so much distrust in the world, so much division, our newscasters reporting another school shooting, another political feud, many of us are in the mood for something else. We want to learn of a little human kindness going around, to hear the good stories that are happening. While it's hard to tell how much trust has eroded, how high anger levels have become these last few years, the world certainly seems a less friendly and more cynical place than it used to be.

What happens to artists when anger, frustration, and doubt are so palpable? The delicate soul of creativity wants to hide. Keep to herself. She needs free, open space to flourish, an energetic spirit that is positive and flowing. But when strong emotions arise and want to dominate our every thought and action, how do we keep them from blocking our creativity? We may need to let off some steam. "Anger is meant to be listened to. Anger is a voice, a shout, a plea, a demand. Anger shows us where we want to go," write Mark Bryan and Julia Cameron in *The Artist's Way at Work*. "In the recovery of a blocked artist, anger is a sign of health."[106] Rather than seeing anger as a positive, however, we often allow increasing tensions to become a barometer of the rising levels of anger and stress in our lives. We see

---

[106] Mark Bryan and Julia Cameron, *The Artist's Way at Work: Riding The Dragon* (New York: HarperCollins, 1999).

the effects, not only in our creativity, but in the very way we live. Instead of seeing possibility, we see roadblocks. We start to distrust our own sense of power, mirroring what we sense in the bigger world. We become anxious and unsettled.

But in spite of the state of the world and our anxiety about it, we must continue to pursue our creative goals and desires. Our artwork may reflect the acrimony and disquiet around us, or it may reflect the beauty that still remains. And so we keep on, accepting our emotions and using them to clarify what's important. As when fire is applied to metal, we can use the heat of our outrage and frustration to laser in on what's significant, helping us shape and refine how we want to respond in the world.

It may frighten you to feel so much passion, but please don't shy away from it. Let anger in your art—in whatever form—be a needed response to injustice and violation. Break the code of silence that is often expected. Take a stand and use the expression of anger to invest in better outcomes for our world. Fabian, a high school senior, did. After learning about the conflict in the Middle East, he became upset, raging, and using acrylics in black, gray, and red, created a throbbing splatter painting he titled "War." The next day it was used as a centerpiece for a meaningful class discussion.

How do your passions direct your art? When we touch the flame of anger, it can bring us, according to David Whyte, "into the world making the mind clearer and more generous, the heart more compassionate, and the body . . . strong enough to handle it."[107] We want to be fully alive in this world, don't we? To love freely and feel deeply, and to allow our art to take us where it is compelled to go.

---

[107] David Whyte, *Consolations: The Solace, Nourishment and Underlying Meaning of Everyday Words* (Langley, WA: Many Rivers Press, 2015).

Accepting Our Gifts

*Believe in yourself. You are braver than you think, more
talented than you know, and capable of more than you
imagine.*

—Roy T. Bennett, *The Light in The Heart*

Many of us find it difficult to accept compliments. "You are so talented," a friend says, or "You look fabulous," and you make a face or shrug it off, unwilling or unable to accept the praise. You read a poem at an open mic and someone tells you how wonderful the poem is, how well you presented it. You smile, but inwardly you think: *It really wasn't that great.*

Why do we do this? Why are we reluctant to accept the gifts we've been given—our abilities in music, the magic we do with words? We believe we are not worthy. We doubt. The inner critic is sometimes so powerful we become blind to our talents.

Or it may be, while inwardly we recognize that we *do* have gifts in certain areas, we fear we won't live up to expectations. Despite an ability to play the violin or the piano, what if we screw up the audition? What if the manuscript our friends consider "so fine" is never published? Potential can be a fearsome thing, and in the face of setbacks that inevitably occur in the creative life, we find it less disappointing if we devalue ourselves, marginalize our abilities.

Sometimes, too, we may feel that our talents don't appear in the form we think they should. Perhaps you have a natural ability in modern dance, but believe that you should be doing ballet. Or that your talent for poetry is "just a little something you do" and if you were really anything, you would write "big, important books" or novels.

Accepting our talents goes along with accepting who we are, and in our culture—especially for women—we have a hard time doing this. We are too tall or too skinny, scatter-brained, our hair too curly or our lips too thin. We see the innate beauty and grace in others but are unwilling to see the same in ourselves.

But we cannot grow and become fully actualized—that is, reach the potential we have within—if we do not accept ourselves as we are, in our physical bodies and in the amazing capabilities bestowed upon us. We are who we are, with our imperfections, yes, but also with our natural talents.

Self-acceptance leads to happiness; and it leads to self-actualization. "We can only be third-rate Alice Munros," my friend likes to say, "but we can be first-rate ourselves." We have been given fabulous gifts, unique to each one of us, and when we accept that and use them, we find more joy in every day, and make the world more vibrant, more marvelous than it already is.

True Grit

A musician must make music, an artist must paint, a poet must write, if he is to be ultimately at peace with himself. What a man can be, he must be.

—Abraham Maslow, *Motivation and Personality*

As writers, we need to do what makes us sing, dance, and from time to time yell, "Oh, Momma!" when the writing goes well. But this is not always the case. Writing is difficult, and at times we have to push uphill, knowing there will be other times we can roll easily back down. Beginning a piece is often difficult, the middle can feel like banging your head against the wall, and then there are the endings. But in order to breathe life into our characters, to edit so each page shines like polished glass, we must be committed and keep working, especially when the going becomes difficult. We have to show true grit.

Sometimes, in the midst of our crazy, upside-down lives, the mere fact of getting to the page can be not only challenging, but heroic. We need to find ways to push the pause button on our lives to slow down, become still enough to string words together. For in order for us to develop our innate talents, to grow, we must keep writing. There are times we will find it impossible to carve out the time we need. When this happens, we must acknowledge, as my grandmother used to say, that "life is full of gives and takes." But we are responsible for our own growth, and as soon as we can, we must begin again. This is true grit.

A couple of years ago at a farmer's market, I noticed a teenage girl sitting at a folding chair with several beautiful charcoal drawings spread in front of her. Sketches of what looked like a family—grandmother, father, mother, and baby brother. They were very detailed with striking contrasts of value, darks and lights, eyes that spoke expression. A crowd gathered, and we watched her dip her head—and, as she was armless—grab a pencil with her mouth and begin to draw, making short pencil strokes, her teeth clenched around the end of the pencil. Someone asked if she thought she'd have been a different artist if she had arms. "I don't know," she replied, "but drawing is so important, I'd have figured out a way."

Ernest Hemingway made a practice of writing no matter where he was—on a fishing cruiser or in a sleeping tent in Africa. During the Spanish Civil War in a city under siege, he wrote his play *The Fifth Column*. Bombs fell in the streets outside his hotel window, and he tapped away at his typewriter. Amidst cannon fire and the whine of high explosive shells, Hemingway kept working. Maybe he did so as a way to find comfort, letting his writing take him to a place of peace even while the country around him raged in war.

Most of us do not have to write while bombs explode around us, but on the journey where writing takes us, we *do* take chances, resurrecting pain from the past, expressing not only the joy but the sorrow that is life. The best efforts often come from writing on the edge. Those who demonstrate this sort of pluck and persistence are the ones we hear about. And the ones we wholeheartedly want to be.

Doing Scary Things

Creativity takes courage.

—Henri Matisse, *Artist to Artist : Inspiration and Advice from Visual Artists Past & Present*

Columnist Mary Schmich said that a worthy goal in living a full life is to "do one thing every day that scares you."[108] Yikes! I don't like the sound of that. But fear is necessary for survival. That's why we don't swim with sharks or drive ninety miles an hour on gravel roads. Of course, there are many things to fear. In my childhood I was afraid of tornados, snakes, burglars, kidnappers, sickness, the ram that chased me around the pasture, and the neighbor's bull, which might.

So I avoid sharks and steer clear of angry bulls; I'm a careful driver and take care of my health. But, as in all things, we must find a balance between keeping safe and finding the strength to live fully. "A ship is safe in a harbor," William G. T. Shedd said, "but that's not what ships are for."[109]

So it is that we are compelled to face our fears, to grow, and to realize the great potential that is our life. We need to do scary things. This means that we need courage to:

- Face the blank page or the blank canvas day after day, even when the words won't come or the painting refuses to take form.

- Be willing to create art around painful subjects and personal vulnerabilities.

---

[108] Mary Schmich, "Advice, like youth, probably just wasted on the young," *Chicago Tribune,* (Chicago, IL) June 1, 1997.

[109] William G.T. Shedd, qtd. by Gary Ninneman, *C.I.A.: Church in Atrophy* (Maitland, FL: Xulon Press, 2006) 167.

- Write badly, paint and sculpt badly. Whatever the art form, consent to do it badly.

- Submit our work for scrutiny (whether it be to an informed colleague, critique group, or to a potential publisher).

- Make a telephone call or send an email as follow-up to a submission.

- Ask for a favor on behalf of our work.

Most of our fears revolve around failure, looking foolish, losing face, and being rejected. These are grownup fears, and we face them every day. I'm not sure I can be as brave as Mary Schmich and do a scary thing *every* day. But perhaps I can do an *uncomfortable* thing every day, and try for something scary once a week.

A writer friend once emailed me that she was "doing something scary" that day, and wanted to report back to me at the end of the afternoon. (She was following up on a submission). I like that idea—enlisting the support of another to help us face what we need to face. Whatever it takes to keep us growing and improving, and living our lives creatively.

Dropping into Flow

In flow . . . creativity goes into overdrive, we feel inspired, and motivation springs forth from within.

—Dragos Bratansanu,
*The Pursuit of Dreams: Claim Your Power,
Follow Your Heart, and Fulfill Your Destiny*

As an artist, you know the times when the work is going well, when all your senses come alive, and you realize intuitively what to do—the shading to make in a charcoal drawing, the next movement in a dance sequence. Perhaps it's the riff in a song you're composing that seems to write itself. At times like these, you are in the flow.

Hungarian psychologist, Mihaly Csikszentmihalyi, developed the theory of flow, describing it as the mental state in which one is "completely involved in an activity for its own sake. The ego falls away. Time flies. Every action, movement, and thought follows inevitably from the previous one, like playing jazz . . ."[110] In flow there's a feeling of near-ecstasy, euphoria, in which whatever you do feels natural and right. Athletes describe this as being "in the zone." Musicians say they are "in the groove." All artists feel this, but it never seems to come often enough.

How can we enter into the state of flow more easily? Csikszentmihalyi said that for flow to occur, two conditions must be present. First of all, we must have sufficient skills in the area in which we are working. And secondly, we must have a worthy challenge. Without the necessary skill, we'll be frustrated, and if the task isn't challenging enough, boredom will set in. Then, within your area of expertise,

[110] Mihaly Csikszentmihalyi, qtd. by Geirland, John, "Go with The Flow," *Wired* 4, no. 9 (September 1996).

choose a goal or task which is *specific and definable*. If you're a poet who's written and published several poems of good quality, set a goal of writing a series of poems. If you're a visual artist who's mastered the basics of perspective and light and shadow, it's time to tackle something more complex such as drawing the human hand.

Next, *start* on the task. Overcome procrastination. It is estimated to take at least fifteen minutes of concentrated work before flow arises. But first, one must *start,* and this may be the most difficult thing of all. We're reluctant to embark on the first hard part; we drag our feet.

But when we do . . . *ah!* Working in a state of flow, not only are we productive and innovative, lost in what we are doing, but we feel happy. Our "best moments," Csikszentmihalyi said, "usually occur when [the] body or mind is stretched to its limits . . . to accomplish something difficult and worthwhile."[111] Striving for flow is one of the best things we can do—for satisfaction and contentment, for quality of life, for sheer joy.

---

[111] Ibid.

For Your Journey

Sometimes we look at the challenges facing us and wonder if we have enough, or if we *are* enough. Are we like the lion in the Wizard of Oz looking every place else for courage instead of within? Or, even worse, the scarecrow looking for brains? Cheri Huber famously said, "How you do anything is how you do everything."[112] What does this mean? It all matters. How we answer the doorbell, how we meet new office mates, how we walk down a street, how we ask for a raise, how we say no. It's essential to connect with our authentic selves, embracing every moment as another opportunity to be honest and brave, conveying, as my grandfather used to say, "mean what you say, say what you mean."

1. "Who Are You" is an activity that lets you reflect on how attitudes influence behaviors. *Select a colleague who manages change well and overcomes challenges with relative ease. Draw two large heads on your paper. One is your chosen colleague and the other, you. Review the following attributes and any others you would like to add, writing down on the profile of your colleague those that fit: holds multiple perspectives, risk taker, believes in possibilities, embraces change, says yes more than no, spends time creating, and sees diversity as a resource. The second head reflects your mental landscape. Write down which attributes from the list you convey. How do you compare? Which ones are similar? Any missing? Identify the attributes that reflect you. Are there any areas you want to grow?*

---

[112] Cheri Huber, *How You Do Anything Is How You Do Everything* (Keep It Simple Books, 1998).

2. The "Stones in Our Path" exercise takes honest, deep reflection, looking into our dark side, our shadow side, uncovering more of ourselves. "Stones" are those things that hold you back. For example, feelings of inferiority, excessive anger or being disorganized. *Find yourself a quiet place and slow down your breath. Consider your habits, lifestyle, and temperament, and reflect upon the stones that work against you, keep you from being your best. Don't dwell on them or beat yourself up about them, just jot down the "stones" that describe you today. Make a list.*

3. Besides impeding your progress, blocking your growth, your stones can serve another purpose: slowing you down to do important interior work. They can help you become more aware of what may be rumbling inside. *Look back over your list and consider any "stones" that may benefit you. If you recognize that you are too angry at times, broaden your perspective to apply both/and thinking. Both of these statements may be true for you. My anger disrupts relationships and affects job performance. But what else may be true? Anger motivates you to stand up for yourself or someone else, apply for another job, be aware inside that something is wrong. Circle the stones on your list which may serve a dual purpose.*

4. Now look at your list. *Sort into two columns those "stones" you want to sustain and those you want to let go. Consider how you are going to let go of those unwanted ones. Visualize them being carried away in a hot air balloon, or tossed in a deep lake. Do it. Now thank yourself for your hard work today.*

PART FOUR:
In the Sweet Spot

I think we each have a personal sweet spot . . . It's the state of mind in which we experience the most joy and satisfaction in being ourselves.

—David Spangler,
Foundational Incarnational Exercises

Chapter Ten:
Build Your Life as an Artist

Seek Your Golden Mean

Don't hurry, don't rest.

—Shinichi Suzuki,
The Suzuki Method

How we spend our days defines who we are. Each day can be a new beginning, an opportunity for creativity and discovery. But whenever we set our schedules *too* rigidly, push too hard, or move too fast, our efforts to lead the lives we want are compromised. The little cubes of day we call life quickly pass. Instead, we need to seek our *golden mean*, the optimum middle place between the two extremes of too much effort to achieve—and too little. We creatives find this golden mean when we experience the optimal tension, the perfect rhythm and flow with our art and are able to make manifest what we've been toiling and aching over. The coy sweet spot resides here.

You know this honeyed place where your art comes alive, where *you* come alive. A place where the imagination is stretched to its limits, where each new encounter seems to explode with ideas like a profusion of musical notes tumbling out one after another. Your versatility may astound you at times—deciding whether or not to add a little gray to make the clouds seem as if you could reach out and touch them, or to change a note in a cello movement. How can you compare—light gray versus gray one shade darker? F versus F sharp? Doesn't inspiration come from nullity, arriving like a wild banshee, a

207

character in your short story no longer mysterious but with shape and form? Is the golden mean at work here?

My friend, an accomplished church organist, after working months on a difficult organ sonata, struggling and despairing, suddenly found herself playing the sonata as she never had before.

"My fingers took over as if they had minds," she said, her voice rising as she told her story. "Magnificent sounds enveloped me, and I played with such joy, masterfully, far beyond my technical ability." Why did it happen, she wondered. What conditions produced this creative miracle so that the free-for-all universe decided to make a visit? Was it the church bells chiming above, streaks of sunlight coming through the multi-colored stained glass windows onto the keys, or was it surrendering after so many months of practice, of such sweet torment? However it happened, Donna had reached her sweet spot, her exalted golden mean, where music spoke to her.

How can you find your golden mean, learn how to enter places in your art-life that lead to such significance? How can you experience more creative abundance? The most important thing, according to Maxine Greene, is "to uncouple from the mundane and the routine" and "perceive the qualities in a play or painting or poem or sonata."[113] You must learn how to listen, to recognize patterns and colors that fill and excite you—to seek words that delight or words that help you discern your sense of place, that evoke the warmth of home, or the shades and nuances of loss and disappointment.

Each person must find her own golden mean. It's individual and personal—the summation of your life's experiences, how your sensory system perceives form and gesture and word, the strength of your attention. All of these combine and combust to usher you to a deeper, more complex world, a world of hard-won creative pursuits.

---

[113] Maxine Greene, *Variations on a Blue Guitar: The Lincoln Center Institute Lectures on Aesthetic Education* (New York: Teachers College Press, 2001).

The Pomodoro Method

Nothing can be done except little by little.

—Charles Baudelaire,
*The Essence of Laughter
and Other Essays, Journals, and Letters*

My writer friend Laurie tells the story of how she adjusted her work schedule, switching her part-time hours to the afternoon so she'd have her mornings free to write. It was going to be wonderful, she told me, but the first morning with three glorious hours stretching out before her, she couldn't seem to get under way. "I couldn't get out of the starting block," she said. "I just sat there." Does this sound familiar at all? It does for me, I know, whether I'm writing poetry, working on new pages of a novel or short story, or writing a potential blog post. It's just hard to get going.

Recently, however, I've discovered an approach that helps. It's called "The Pomodoro Method," a technique developed by Francesco Cirillo that can help writers, visual artists, *any* artist overcome inertia and be more productive.[114] And most importantly, it serves to *rewire* the brain around your creative goals. But what is a Pomodoro? And what is "The Pomodoro Method?" A pomodoro is a type of Italian tomato, and the Pomodoro Method (which gets its name from a kitchen timer shaped like a tomato) is a way to use time more effectively. To use this technique, set a timer for twenty-five minutes, focus on the task at hand, and work until the timer signals you can stop. *It's only twenty-five minutes*, you tell yourself, *I can work for twenty-five minutes*. And

---

[114] Francesco Cirillo, *The Pomodoro Technique: The Life-Changing Time-Management System* (London: Ebury Publishing, 2018).

so you do, soon finding yourself absorbed in your work, and a little dismayed when the timer sounds.

The idea is that *you begin*. And when faced with a big project—like a novel, a series of sketches, or selecting and mounting pictures for a photography exhibit, it helps to divide your work time into smaller bits so that you center yourself, really zero in on the task before you. And twenty-five minutes is a good amount of time to immerse yourself into the work before your brain cries out for time off.

When first beginning with this approach, you may want to start small. Try completing three Pomodoros a day—that is, three twenty-five-minute increments of time separated by a five-minute break. It's important not to skip the break and to stay focused during the twenty-five minutes of work time. Don't answer the phone, check Facebook or e-mail; keep to the task, and if interrupted, start the timer again. At the end of that time, you will find you've made real progress.

What is intriguing is that when we use the Pomodoro Method (in addition to being better able to start working), we are re-wiring our brains to focus *intently*—one small increment of time after another. We're actually training ourselves to concentrate better; and in a world where distractions are all around us, that's important. Let's say you want to complete a twelve page chapter by the end of the week. That's a great goal, and a doable one—but there is still the challenge of getting to the page. Start with three Pomodoros first thing in the morning, that is *work, break, work, break, work, break*—then take a longer break. And if your brain is up to the task, do another three.

Jason Calacanis said, "You have to have a big vision and take very small steps to get there."[115] Writing a book or completing a number of designs for a fashion show are big visions. Using the Pomodoro Method, one twenty-five-minute block at a time, can help turn them into reality.

---

[115] Jason Calacanis, "7 Voices of Transformation: Interviews with Security Awareness Vendors." *O'Reilly.com*.

Curiosity and the Gaze

I have no special talents.
I am only passionately curious.

—Albert Einstein, *Letter to Carl Seelig*

Visual artists often talk about deepening their curiosity by using the *gaze*. Looking at something without flinching. When we study compositions or objects, the images and colors may shift like a child's kaleidoscope. Complex shapes emerge, and something inside clicks like a key opening a door. And that which was locked away becomes recognizable. You stare at the composition, look deeper, and continue to hold that pose until you feel a movement in your chest. Your heart rate increases. There's a connection between object and feeling, an inner exchange that takes place. Consider, for example, da Vinci's *Mona Lisa.* What does her smile say to you? Is she radiant or expressing seriousness? When you keep looking, does her affect seem to change?

Not long ago, I had the opportunity to study Michelangelo's *David* in a gallery in Italy. At first glance, I saw his worried brow, the tension of the muscles in his lips and face, how his eyes locked in the distance—perhaps searching for Goliath. Then I looked at the sculpture with a long gaze. David's beautiful, muscular body, in contrast to his expression, seemed relaxed, his sling resting casually on his shoulder. What was he communicating?

Taking in this masterpiece, different feelings emerge. Certainly, we experience the universal appeal of the engaging composition, but there's more. We feel respect and admiration for the young hero, his image symbolic of how a different outcome can result *if* we bring new courage and critical thinking to a situation, even in the face of seemingly impossible odds. "Whatever you're meant to do, do it now," Doris Lessing reminds us. "The conditions are always impossible."[116]

As for me, I'm not facing actual giants, although it feels like that when I'm in a challenging work situation or frustrated with my art. But the image of David reminds me that the most important action we can take is to do our best. Everyone has difficult rivers to navigate—glass ceilings to crack, overwhelming family obligations—but like *David*, when we use the gaze, looking at our challenges without flinching, we see what we may have missed before. And when we deploy all our skills and talents, what we accomplish can be amazing.

---

[116] Doris Lessing, *The Grass Is Singing* (London: Michael Joseph Ltd., 1950).

How Do We Write?

*Creativity is a habit, and the best creativity is a result
of good work habits. That's it in a nutshell.*

—Twyla Tharp,
The Creative Habit: Learn It and Use It for Life

So many writers I read about rise at four or five o'clock every day; get up to a cold, dark house; go to their computers; and write five hundred or so words before breakfast. I think about that and despair. I can't do that. It's just not in my makeup; and if getting up in the wee hours is one of the requirements to be a writer, I'm not going to make it. So when I read that one of Susan Sontag's resolutions had been to start getting up every day *by eight o'clock*—so as to get to her writing desk earlier, I was relieved.

I think we know in our bones that there is no one "right" way to write, that each writer has his or her own way of approaching the blank page, his or her own habits and rituals that make up their writing lives—but it's good to be reminded of that once in a while. That how and when we write, and with what quirky habits, is just fine. I remember Kent Haruf—late great Colorado and Nebraska novelist—saying that he wrote in his basement before a blank wall, pecking away at his keyboard wearing gloves with the fingertips cut out. Hemingway wrote while standing. Besides rising by eight, Susan Sontag wrote "with a felt-tip pen, or sometimes a pencil, on yellow or white legal pads . . ." liking "the slowness of writing by hand."[117]

In regards to my writing friends, Gina enjoys writing in a recliner or her adjustable bed. Marge also likes to write in bed, and besides

---

[117] Susan Sontag, Interview by Edward Hirsch, "Susan Sontag, The Art of Fiction No. 143," *The Paris Review* 137 (Winter 1995).

that, likes to "write with a friend." Barbara finds ways to "get in a place where I'm not thinking," and writes in a blank notebook.

I love hearing about how other writers structure their days to get ink down on paper, what special habits they've adopted; and I believe that most writers share this fascination. It's almost as if we are looking for the recipe, the step-by-step instructions as to how we can write more—how we can write up to our potential.

We realize, of course, that success lies not in the particular habit or ritual we adopt, but in perseverance. Keeping at the task and not giving up. Holding it close. According to Ray Bradbury, love is the key. "Fall in love and stay in love. Write only what you love, and love what you write. They key word is love. You have to get up in the morning and write something you love, something to live for."[118]

So, whenever and however you write, with pen or pencil or computer, on yellow legal pads or the backs of envelopes, with someone else or alone . . . do it steadily and faithfully, and do it with love.

---

[118] Ray Bradbury, qtd. by Gene Beley, *Ray Bradbury Uncensored! the Unauthorized Biography* (Lincoln: iUniverse, 2006).

Getting a New Outlook

*Renewal requires opening yourself to new ways of
thinking and feeling.*

—Deborah Day, *Be Happy Now!*
Become the Active Director of Your Life

Every summer, my husband and I travel to the sandhills of Nebraska
where Tom attends Bluegrass Camp. We rent a cabin along Pine
Creek, and evenings sit and listen to the water gurgling and trickling
along. From the trees, the red-eyed vireo makes its three-note call.
Three notes, another three notes, then two. Over and over he calls. We
hear robins and killdeer, finches and mourning doves, and as it gets
darker, the high-pitched trill of the nighthawk. Sometimes we track
a storm building in the west—watch forks of lightning criss-crossing
the sky.

In the morning, Tom packs up his banjo and mandolin and heads
for his music session. I sit on the porch and read or write. It is a beautiful porch. The cabin owner, Nancy, is a woman who knows how
to put together wicker furniture, palm trees, Japanese lanterns, and
candles to create a setting in which it is a delight to sit and relax. To
sip coffee and listen to my husband and his friends pluck the strings on
their instruments, try out the new songs they've written.

We are so lucky to live in all the richness that surrounds us and
realize the possibilities here for us to explore. Possibilities that have
been here all along, but which we often overlook, busy with the
everyday of our lives. When we step out of the everyday, however,
we have the opportunity to see the world with fresh eyes. That's what
it's like for me during my week or two in the sandhills. The new
surroundings give me new ideas. When I go home, I'm energized,

wanting to make changes to my *own* front porch—make it more inviting, a more pleasant haven. And since I'm a writer, I want to write some new stories, new poems.

Even back home, there are ways to continue that "vacation feeling," that feeling of being away from everything—no matter where you are. Consider these:

- Move away from the routines of your life and open up space for what truly matters. Spend your time doing what makes you come alive—writing, painting, walking in nature.

- Visit a Garden Center or Outdoor Living store. Look for flowers and plants that delight you; breathe in their sweet scent, and consider a project (or a purchase) that can enhance your time outdoors.

- It has been said that blue is the color most associated with enhanced creativity. Get out your blue rugs, your blue dishes and glassware. Take a walk under the blue sky, and really notice what you see.

"The secret to a rich life is to have more beginnings than endings," Dave Weinbaum said.[119] We can do that every day.

---

[119] Dave Weinbaum, "The secret to a rich life is to have more beginnings than endings," *Jewish World Review* (July 14, 2017). Web.

Artists' Sanctuaries

Barack, I've come to understand, is the sort of person who needs a hole, a closed-off little warren where he can read and write undisturbed.

—Michelle Obama, *Becoming*

Artists have always used whatever nook or cranny is available in order to create, spend time alone, and explore the world of the imagination. Many re-order a room in their home to call their own, a private realm to paint, write, make and do. This could be a library, den, or second-floor bedroom tweaked to fit specific creative needs. My musician-writer-artist friend Pam has a "guest room" and a "piano room" she calls her "comfortable dream spaces." These rooms feature a grand piano as well as an upright, bookshelves of piano music, a bass guitar, mandolin, an art table overlooking a busy birdfeeder, and three great views of her lovely backyard.

For those who want space separate from their living quarters, an "artist shed" may be the answer. This can be built or converted from an existing structure and placed at the back of your yard, or within the tangle of an overgrown garden. Perhaps hidden so well that, in passing, you wonder if it is there at all, the privacy enabling you to get in touch with your own creative force and with the rhythms of nature. Stepping through the door of your sanctuary can be like boarding a train and disappearing for a while. And when you return, you may not recognize yourself any longer. As Thomas Merton observed, "Art enables us to find ourselves and lose ourselves at the same time."[120]

Shed creations reflect an artist's lifestyle, sense of play and evolving aspirations. My son-in-law, Chris, built his shed slowly, letting

---

[120] Thomas Merton, *No Man Is an Island* (San Diego: Harcourt & Brace, 2002).

the design and measurements marinate and then take shape in his journal. Large windows facing south and east invite the sunlight in, and a corrugated tin roof allows him to listen to the "percussion of a storm against the roof."

Inside, the wood is bare save for a postcard of Thoreau's cabin nailed into the frame of an old farmhouse window. And outside the window is the garden. "When the weather is warm, I watch day by day as a creeping rose bush consumes and fills the once-bare view," Chris says. "The apple tree shoots buds, blossoms, and the small fruit appears. I see anew with the eyes of an artist."

My artist friend Jude created a place of refuge in the empty space above her detached garage, where she can write, meditate, and paint. When ascending the wrought-iron, winding staircase to the sanctuary she named *Treehouse*, you imagine you're climbing an old oak, feeling the wind on your face, and hearing the happy sounds of chickadees and cardinals. Inside, dark wood timbers spire to a peak, and it is as if you're looking up through a tall tree's branches. A comfortable ochre couch and canvas sling chairs wait invitingly. There are books of all sizes, papers, maps, an Indian Head lamp, framed prints of trees, and flowering begonias. In the corner stands an easel with a painting in process—a meadowlark—and a scattering of tubes of paints.

Artists' sanctuaries are for painting, writing, sculpting, print-making—whatever imaginative endeavors you fancy. But most importantly, they are also for dreaming of what can be.

A Creative Retreat

*In order to understand the world, one has to turn away
from it on occasion.*

—Albert Camus, *The Minotaur*

From time to time, it's a delight to escape from the routine in order to reinvigorate ourselves and to spend dedicated time focused on our creativity. If you were planning the perfect retreat, where would you go? To a friend's cabin in the mountains? A Benedictine monastery?

One of my favorite retreats took place a few years ago with four writing friends on a ranch in northern Nebraska. It was October, and we were lucky enough to experience perfect weather—crisp air, clear blue skies, and gorgeous sunrises and sunsets over unbelievably broad horizons. The prairie was turning beautiful shades of gold and tan and white. Coyotes yipped at dusk, and we saw wild turkeys, deer, Snow Geese. Once we heard the trill of sandhill cranes and looked up to see them flying high overhead, intent on what was within them, what was inherent in them to do. As we writers were.

At this retreat, the major guideline was for there to be silence until four p.m., and so we honored that, each of us writing in our various favorite places—on the porch with a laptop on our knees, at the dining room table, or holed up in our rooms. We raided the refrigerator for breakfasts and lunches, munching bagels or slurping down soup as we wrote. Sometimes we took breaks and walked out on the prairie, teasing out plot lines or just allowing nature to do its wonderful work on us. We struggled with stories and novels, planted a few seeds of poetry. One writer/painter worked on essays and watercolors. We wrote and kept silent, doing what we wanted and needed to do.

You may ask about the no-talking rule. Okay, we cheated a little on that. We whispered, "Is there coffee?" and "Look! Wild turkeys!" But mostly, we were silent until four when we prepared and ate our evening meal together, then shared what we had written that day. Retreats like this are a luxury. Then we go back to our real lives and wonder when we will be able to carve out such a sweet amount of writing time again. It's important, though, to try to uncover "away" time as often as we can—even if it's on a smaller scale.

Perhaps a friend has a vacation home you could use. An empty apartment. Consider a "Home Creative Retreat Day" or "Writing Retreat Weekend," and spend that day or two in a time of sanctuary, a time to devote to what makes you come alive. Stock up on deli food, and write or make music, paint or create woven wall hangings. If you live with another, plan your retreat for a time they will be away so you can have uninterrupted silence. Or go to a motel or a cabin at a state park. Do the retreat solo or get together with another artist or writing friend or two and plan the retreat together. It's not the setting that makes a retreat work, but the state of mind, and the opportunity to focus on using your time and energy to your creative work.

Reverence for the Particular

Life is not a plot: it's in the details.
—Jodi Picoult, *Vanishing Acts*

The essence of creation is awe-inspiring, mysterious, and is steeped in a reverence for the particular. That is, *this* particular red squirrel with its distinctive brushy tail and ear tufts, *that* prairie bluestem, its three-part seed heads nodding in the sun. Creativity insists upon a specific color, angled line, or particular edge of shadow blurred just so. And when we connect to the power and specificity of creation, infusing ourselves with its raw energy, we are carried wherever whimsy wants. Able to access the unique experiences of our lives and bring new creations into the world—specific, one-of-a-kind creations. Only you experience life in the ways you do, and no one can create like you.

With the might of creativity at our side, we find there's always more to offer, more to uncover. It's exhilarating. Whenever we take a detailed look at something, beginning with the particular, the concrete—"just this!"—we open to a new world. We slow down, allow the mind to explore a single gesture, scene, or moment in time, and in so doing, create pathways to new possibilities. It changes how we connect with the world, seeing it not through abstractions or broad philosophies, but rather, as it is, with surplus and distinction.

Sensory details let us share in another person's day-to-day reality by triggering a range of emotions, giving us the power to feel meaning and connection. Artists revel in the particular. A painter picks up her sketch pad and notices the heart shape of the model's lips, the little imperfection at the left corner. Another artist, a potter at the beach, studies waves coming in to shore—the distinctive curl as the wave crests, the gleam of white froth—and later tries to replicate it in earthenware.

In the poem "Abandoned Farmhouse," Ted Kooser uses phrases such as "the bedroom wall papered in lilacs" and "the Bible with a broken back" to trigger feeling responses. These are highly-charged, *specific* words, which stir strong emotional fire and travel straight to the heart. The winters were cold, the poem continues, and there were "rags in the window frames." And "it was lonely," the "narrow country road," seldom traveled.[121] We feel that cold, that loneliness.

Why do artists work so hard for the particular? We want to do our best to communicate the feeling, the terror, the joy that *we* experience. This is what artists do—we reach out to others through our personally wrought creations, wanting more than anything to make a real connection—to offer our hand—making our way, finally, into another's heart.

---

[121] Ted Kooser, "Abandoned Farmhouse," *Sure Signs: New and Selected Poems* (Pittsburgh: University of Pittsburgh Press, 1980).

Because Words Matter

Handle them carefully, for words have more power than atom bombs.

—Pearl Strachan Hurd, *attributed*

Some time ago, while I was editing, going through the so-so manuscript of my novel and trying to make it better, a friend e-mailed to ask how things were going. Before responding, I considered how I'd describe my process. *I'm whipping it into shape,* I thought. But immediately, I took myself in hand. No. Not "whipping." That was too harsh a word for the time I spent with each chapter. And in any event, not very effective.

Words matter. How we talk to others and how we talk to ourselves. How we talk about our art. So no, I didn't want to whip my manuscript into shape, flog my poor story into some sort of submission. First of all, I don't believe that works. Besides, the process of revision is entirely different. So, when thinking and speaking about our work, let's use different words. Let's:

- *Refine* to make our work more detailed, as writers do—instead of referencing "trees" in the distance, substitute more specific words—"ash and cottonwoods."

- *Enhance* to add nuance and depth as a painter might, adding detail to an oil painting of a young girl so that we see a scratch on her arm, a speck on her shirt.

- *Revise,* meaning taking the time to *re-vision* a manuscript, looking at it from different angles, peering into characters' backstories to see what's been missed.

• And lastly, *nudge* works of art to their best, capturing the emotion in a painting or poem.

When I was a little girl, my family had a quarter horse, Fudge, and while my three sisters were superb horsewomen, I wasn't. Fudge took me beneath the low-hanging branches of the locust trees. Another time, on a little canter under the clothesline, he went wherever he wanted to.

Sometimes that's what editing is like, trying to hang onto a huge beautiful animal and coax it along. Make for a glorious ride. A work of art has a heart that makes it what it is. Our job as artists is to guide it on its way, apply a gentle rein, and take care with its heart. And when tough love is required and a need arises to eliminate words, whole paragraphs, or scenes, let's not think of it as "cutting," or "slashing" but clearing away obstacles, making things better for the heart.

This is more than just playing around with word choice. Words have power and energy, and just as we need to speak carefully to nurture our human relationships, so should we when we speak about our art.

The Three Elements

Let the world burn through you. Throw the prism light, white hot, on paper.

—Ray Bradbury, *Zen and the Art of Writing: Releasing the Creative Genius Within You*

Bill Kloefkorn, Nebraska's beloved late state poet, once told a roomful of students that there are three things every writer needs in order to write successfully. I wasn't fortunate enough to be one of those in the room that day, but when a friend began to relate the story to me, I listened with bated breath. Whatever those three elements were, I wanted them. What you need, Kloefkorn explained, are (1) experiences, (2) a lexicon, and (3) passion.

I've thought a lot about that statement, trying to apply it to my own life, and within those words find a great deal of comfort. The three elements described are very much attainable; in fact, it is quite likely that we are *already* in possession of them all. Every time we go out the front door, the world with its wealth of possibility is waiting, and each day our stockpile of experience grows. In regards to a lexicon (a vocabulary), the more we read, talk with friends, watch movies, and listen to music, the greater our bank account of words becomes. The first two elements are essentially given to us, and as time goes by, we grow richer in both.

The third requirement is more difficult to quantify. Passion is not something we go about learning or developing. It comes from within, and when we are in possession of it, we can do almost anything. Georg Wilhelm Frederic Hegel believed that "Nothing great in the world has

225

ever been accomplished without passion."[122] When you are passionate about something, it is like having a great love affair. You are energized, excited, new meaning exists in your life, and every day you awake on fire to be alive and so much in love. When you are passionate about writing, you feel the same way. You want to spend time with what you love, get to know every nuance of the writing process; you work and pray and hope and dream. You have such spirit, such drive, and such energy is devoted to your passion that your writing abilities cannot help but thrive and grow.

It's interesting what Bill Kloefkorn did *not* include on the list. He didn't include the need for an "innate talent" (whatever that might be) or a genius-level IQ, and he didn't say you needed a secluded cabin and large blocks of unscheduled time. We can take heart. What we need is what we already have—experiences, words to describe them, and the deep-down desire, the passion to write.

---

[122] Georg Wilhelm Friedrich Hegel and Johannes Hoffmeister, *Lectures on the Philosophy of World History*, (Cambridge: Cambridge University Press, 1975).

For Your Journey

If you want to be an artist, you must commit to living the life of one. Creative work requires a faithfulness as reliable as the earth's rotation around the sun. Unfortunately, there's not a template for living the artist's life—all of us have unique patterns and ways of being. The work is yours, and yours alone. But first, you must have faith. Faith in the unknown, in your deep wells of imagination, and the world of inspiration. Deep down, we know living passionately requires risks, dipping into ourselves, searching for answers. But our questions keep coming. *How will I inhabit my artist life? Will I find what I need in myself? How do I become friends with the company of solitude?* Consider the wise words of Rainer Maria Rilke: "Live the questions now. Perhaps you will then, gradually, without noticing it, live along some distant day into the answer."[123]

1. Pretend for a week that your nephew is required to complete a short video on the life of an individual. *For seven days, he must film selective moments, including conversations in a person's day. You are asked to participate based on the following conditions: a) during waking hours; b) your regular daily schedule needs to be followed; and c) privacy is respected. At the conclusion of the week's taping, what do you think you learned about how you spend your time? Were there scheduled opportunities for your creative life? What feelings or emotions arose for you? Did you find space and time for your art?*

2. Nearly every aspect of how we think about ourselves is affected by the power of our beliefs. According to Carol Dweck, these

---

[123] Rainer Maria Rilke, *Letter Four* (16 July 1903).

two different ways of being, a fixed mindset and a growth mindset, determine how you see success and failure in your professional and personal lives. A fixed mindset assumes that character, intelligence, and creative ability are unchanging. With this mindset, an individual believes that there is a set amount in these areas, and neither time nor learning will successfully impact them. A growth mindset is the opposite. An individual with a growth mindset loves challenges, and sees failure not as a lack of intelligence, but as an opportunity to change and grow and learn more. This mindset allows individuals to believe in the value of effort and the ability to change personal habits and thinking. *How do you view yourself? If you think your innate ability as an artist is limited and there's little hope for improvement, what can you do to change your mindset? Where do effort, further schooling, or mentoring factor in?*

3. Not all of us can have a special artist's shed, or coveted hideaway to do our art. *If you are without a place of your own, consider creating one. A place where solitude thrums with rapt, wordless attention. Look for unlikely places in your home. A storage area, the furnace room, a little used second or third bedroom. Make at least a corner of the room yours. Draw a blueprint of what your artist home would look like. Consider color, texture, light. Would there be posters, artifacts, cloth hangings, music? Let your passion guide you like falling into your lover's arms, trusting in the possibility of new beginnings.*

Chapter Eleven:
Finding Your Rhythms

The Cycle of Life, of Creativity

Nature is ever at work building and pulling down, creating and destroying, keeping everything whirling and flowing, allowing no rest but in rhythmical motion, chasing everything in endless song out of one beautiful form into another.

—John Muir, *Our National Parks*

A few years ago, hiking on a favorite mountain trail, it seemed that a gigantic game of pick-up-sticks had gone haywire. Piles of pine trunks lay scattered about, dead trees heaped up one on another. There were ponderosa, lodgepole, Scotch and limber pine—once magnificent specimens towering eighty to ninety feet, now victims to the mountain tree beetle and hewed down by lumberjacks. But farther up the path, a colony of new trees arced upwards, one through the sprawl of a giant fallen log, its branches twisted and pressed under the tree's great weight, and yet thriving. Open now to sunshine, young aspen reached to the sky, and ferns popped like mushrooms, the forest demanding new life.

This is the natural world where the cycle of life, death, and rebirth is written into the DNA of every living thing. Artists, too, follow a similar cycle. We are caretakers of our passions and create around its seasons, sifting through our work to determine what we want to nurture and what must be put aside. We are inspired, we grow and flourish. Then, inevitably, we hit a brick wall and collapse.

But like the pine forest, gradually we find ourselves opening, discovering untapped reserves, and are renewed. And we begin working again. The brick wall is a natural part of the artistic journey, and times of dissatisfaction and low energy are to be expected. It is at these times that we need to be patient, look for new ways into our work, and ride out the cycle.

One day, during a slow period of creativity, I was enjoying myself at a local art gallery when I was taken with a painting of an old woman in a blue dress. The painting reminded me of my grandmother in her favorite blue apron, and I rushed home to finish a poem that had been under construction for some time. I didn't visit the art gallery with the goal of finishing the poem. I went there to see what would become visible to me, what would get my attention. As Margaret Sackville said, "Great imaginations are apt to work from hints and suggestions."[124] I took the hint, the suggestion, and found my way back to creativity, discovering again that great contentment.

---

[124] Margaret Sackville, qtd. by Susan Ferrier, *The Works of Susan Ferrier* (New York: AMS Press, 1970).

Out of the Everyday

Extraordinary magic is woven through ordinary life. Look around!

—Amy Leigh Mercree, *A Little Bit of Meditation*

Always I have loved reading and writing—poetry especially, and as a girl and young woman, I wrote a great deal. Then life intervened with its busy-ness, and I stopped writing. Deep down I was discouraged, thinking I wasn't very good, that I didn't really have anything to write about—nothing very interesting, anyway. So why try?

The writing bug was still in me, however, and after being away from Nebraska for a long time, I moved back and picked up some books by Plains poets, Bill Kloefkorn and Ted Kooser. Immediately, I was drawn back into the magic of writing. I read poems about peeling potatoes and milking cows, one about a dead mouse on the floor of a parking garage, another about a young farmer's satisfaction in his baby, "solid as a tractor lug."[125] These seemed to me rather ordinary subjects to be writing about. But the poems themselves! They were moving, evocative, creating pictures in the mind. Reading them, it was as if the wind had suddenly changed direction. Maybe it's all right to write about everyday things, I thought. Things remembered from my childhood—like the sound a windmill makes when the wind starts up, or walking to school worrying about long division. Everyday, but intriguing.

After all, the ordinariness of life is wonderful, isn't it? Looking out at the garden to ordinary yarrow growing with its lacy leaves, its clusters of gold blossoms. There is bee balm—red and pink, roses and

---

[125] Bill Kloefkorn, "#11," *Alvin Turner as Farmer* (Wayne, NE: Logan House Press, 2004).

231

daylilies. Common enough flowers. A little breeze blows and everyday clouds float overhead. But it's a perfectly marvelous day.

Maybe our very best art has its origins in the everyday. We all have heard the advice, "write what you know." Donald Hall wrote about horses, Jane Kenyon about "mud season" and "the coldest imaginable ooze."[126] Anne Sexton wrote one of my favorite poems, "Welcome Morning," about the joy she found in her morning routine. In reading these poems, we see that what we consider as ordinary can be, in fact, absolutely amazing. That we are able to discover this in the writing process is a privilege and a delight, and one of the great side-benefits of living a creative life.

---

[126] Jane Kenyon, "Mud Season," *Ploughshares* (Summer/Fall 1982).

The Close Dance of Structure and Freedom

I thrive on structure. I find my freedom in structure.
—Lupita Nyong'o, interview in ET Canada

Little do we value as much as freedom—freedom to think and feel what we want, to make our own choices, even to make our own mistakes. And in our creative lives, freedom is the open door we walk through to possibility.

Most of the poetry I read is written in free verse—as is what I write—the lines unencumbered with requirements of meter, rhyme or stanza structure, the words flowing as they will, whatever wants to rise to the surface allowed to do so. Currently, it is the generally accepted poetic form, but it was not always so. Robert Frost said, "Writing free verse is like playing tennis with the net down,"[127] and G. K. Chesterton held that free verse "is not a new metre any more than sleeping in a ditch is a new school of architecture."[128]

For many of us, free verse seems more egalitarian, more accessible. But even with its lack of restraint, its marvelous freedom, the poem must still do its job—shining a light on truth in a new way, evoking feeling and emotion. Always, we must find a way to write "good poems," and in this, structure can help.

Creative breakthroughs often involve some element of constraint. When writing a haiku or sonnet, the particular structure presents a check, a restriction which can give rise to surprising moments. If you need to find a word with a certain number of syllables, say, or to form

---

[127] Robert Frost, Address at Milton Academy, Massachusetts (17 May 1935).

[128] G.K. Chesterton, *Fancies Versus Fads* (New York: Dodd, Mead & Co., 1923).

a four-line stanza, you turn away from the easy, most obvious choice to something new, perhaps something stunning.

For many years I have led generative writing groups—that is, groups which meet for the express purpose of generating new writing. We use writing exercises, and often come up with word lists, from which, in our writing time, we're encouraged to select two or three words to use in what we write. This provides a constraint. We also have the constraint of a time limit—in our group about twenty minutes—in which we are to write "something." With these self-imposed restrictions, it almost always happens that the group does in fact write, and write well—the structure, the constraint working to free the mind.

It's an irony, isn't it, that with restraint we are at liberty to create as we choose, as we never would have imagined. In limitations we find a new kind of freedom, creativity blossoming even with impediments, perhaps *because of* the impediments. We all use structure. Visual artists make sketches, musicians establish song arrangements, novelists write one chapter, then another and another. We devote our mornings to art, afternoons to the world's work—bringing in income and caring for one another. "The universe is built on a plan," Paul Valery said. "The profound symmetry of which is somehow present in the inner structure of our intellect."[129] It is also present in the way we create.

Of course we know that creativity is about letting go, surrendering, allowing mystery to come out of the mists and make itself clear. The key in finding the mystery is in the balance between structure and freedom, that close dance.

---

[129] Paul Valery, qtd. by Timothy Ferris, *The Coming of Age in the Milky Way* (New York: HarperCollins, 2003).

Revel in the Game of Life

Nature is very much alive. Intelligent living beings and vibrant energies are all over the planet.

—Sun Bear, *Walk in Balance:*
The Path to Healthy, Happy, Harmonious Living

Driving east on Interstate 80 towards Lincoln, Nebraska, I first saw them—in pairs, then trios—then a large squadron of sandhill cranes—punctuating the yellowing sky with a low roar. The echoes of the cranes' trumpeting voices are as evocative of Nebraska as the song of the western meadowlark, or the cry of a coyote, their calls, as naturalist Paul A. Johnsgard describes them, the "music of an angelic avian chorus."[130] The sound, visceral, ancient, enters my whole body.

The cranes' annual visit to the Platte River is an early sign of spring. Their constant clamoring as much about the changing of seasons as the gentle blue and yellow crocuses poking their heads through the earth, or the trills of the first robins.

My painter friend, Meredith, also feels the madness of spring, its exaltation, when skies burn deep with a radiant pink. Spring, for her, is the season of irrepressible desire. She goes to her easel, dusts off the tubes of paint, and waits. She senses the image of something beautiful, something strong and true taking form in her mind, feels the colors of alizarin crimson, ultramarine blue, cadmium yellow beckoning. Guided by some invisible power, she creates a design, spreading colors like the northern lights across the canvas before her.

In *The Art of Possibility*, Rosamund and Benjamin Zander describe two steps for finding the spark of creativity. The first is to let

---

[130] Paul A. Johnsgard, *A Chorus of Cranes: The Cranes of North America and the World* (Boulder, CO: University Press of Colorado, 2015).

go, and "let the vital energy of passion surge through you."[131] The second is to participate fully, allowing yourself to be the conduit for "a new expression in the world."

Creativity flows when we allow ourselves to be part of the natural life force, whatever season we're in. I like watching my friend Francis play the violin—Minuet in G by Beethoven—and am transfixed by the lightness of his face, the exquisite beauty of his playing. Maybe, that's what participating fully means—opening up to the energy of our music, our watercolors, whatever bewitches us, reveling in the game of life and finding our own unique expression in the world.

As we drove with our backs to the setting sun, I noticed a large lake where birds were settling for the night, the surface of the water almost completely covered with the textured, moving bodies of tens of thousands of cranes. I felt so happy I was almost dizzy watching their graceful rising and falling, disappearing and re-appearing in the rich, rousing maelstrom as if they too were expressing their delight in the ancient game called life.

How are you participating in life? Are you clamoring and climbing too? Trying to create as a working artist a particular memory, a fresh perspective? Connect with the river of life, let it move in and through and around you, and be the conduit for something new and beautiful to be born upon the earth.

---

[131] Rosamund and Benjamin Zander, *The Art of Possibility* (New York: Penguin Books, 2002).

Linked through Rhythm

Dance is creativity in motion.

—Anonymous

There are those who write poetry and sing arias, those who play the guitar or paint bowls of fruit, and then there are those whose bodies become instruments for beauty and creativity. The ones who love to tap their feet or swing their hips, perform en pointe in ballet. When we allow our bodies to express what we feel, it's magic, sublime. Dance is inexpressible beauty, creativity in movement. Some lucky families are linked through the experience of dancing, of finding themselves so immersed in music, they can't help but move to its rhythms.

My grandparents' passion for "cutting the rug" is part of the family folklore. Grandfather Will was over six foot, had jet black hair and a smile so infectious he couldn't help but attract the attention of the ladies at the Lutheran church social, including my blue-eyed Grandmother Ella. The story goes that someone started strumming a guitar, and my grandfather, despite knowing that the church didn't allow dancing, proclaimed that "Surely God wants us to do something with our legs besides tramping through cornfields!" So, in front of the startled parishioners, he strode over to Ella, extended his hand, and waltzed her around the church lawn.

Grandfather Will passed on his love for dance to my father—who said there were times he just felt the "itch"—and along with my mother, jitterbugged into several dance contests. Dance was a way for them to leave behind routine and hardship for a time, and during especially low times on the farm, escape into a place outside themselves—into movement and the thrum of music, an exhilarating world where jive was king. I still remember watching them do their routines: their famous "Between the Legs Dip," then the "Spin in the Air," Mom landing on her feet, nearly in a backbend, jazz hands shaking.

There's an imaginary string that runs from my grandparents and parents, then through me to my daughters and granddaughters. The string connects us in many ways—love of animals, good books, starlit nights—but most of all, dancing: the passion for movement transmitted like an unseen electrical impulse sending Morse code messages. "Feel it! Feel it!" the messages seem to say, "shape your body around the beat!" Elegance isn't required, but we must *move*. Dance is one of the ways we create, using our arms, legs, and bodies to tell a story, express a mood, find space in the world.

Did dance choose us? Or did we choose dance? We don't know. Why are any of us blessed with an art form that inhabits us, guides our hands, instills in our voices the ability to make sweet melodies? That allows us to see different shades of gold or understand how sunlight affects a subject? We are complex human beings with multiple, often untapped talents.

There's a fire inside you waiting to be stoked. But first you have to notice the ember of longing, a desire. Listen, pay attention. Feed that desire. Kick up your heels. Find something that brings you a sense of jubilation. I hope it's dance.

Time Travel

When you practice quieting your mind and forcing yourself to be Still, you open yourself to the truly limitless creative power within the universe.

—The Stillness Project

In Thornton Wilder's play, *Our Town*, Emily, who has recently died in childbirth, comes back to earth to revisit her past for one day and is overcome by the blindness with which everyone goes through their lives. While the play was written over seventy-five years ago, we may face an even harder time today seeing each other, focusing on what is right in front of our eyes. This has profound implications. Daniel Goleman, in *Focus: The Hidden Driver of Excellence*, contends that learning to pay attention is connected to our emotional intelligence and well-being. It can also affect our creativity.

According to Goleman, being able to detach from everyday distractions requires the discipline of focus. When we practice this habit of the mind—when we slow down and recognize the goodness in every day, not only do we experience delight and spontaneity, we increase our chances to be creative. In order to develop focus, we must learn to pay attention. Time of day matters. The relationship between focus and creativity and our body clock is well established—every person has his own peak schedule to be creative. Optimal creativity has to do with one's energy levels and ability to concentrate. How alert are you in the morning? What is your energy like in the afternoon? When you pay attention to your body's natural rhythms, you do your best creative work.

One sunny morning, my mind quiet, my thoughts floating back and forth in time, I turned my attention to a pot of begonias by my

239

window. How many small blooms made up the beautiful crested mounds, I wondered. Looking closely, small features became visible: two rectangular-shaped holes in one of the leaves, a spider's tiny, fine lines, and on one mound, blossoms looking like a small chorus of children's faces. Suddenly, I was traveling back in time and seeing an old black-and-white school photograph—my first-grade class at Athens Elementary, all giggles and shyness.

How do we learn to pay attention and find the richness which is all around us? Three ways. The first step involves self-awareness. Reflect on your day and find those moments you are most curious and open, relaxed, yet alert. Set your creative clock around this rhythm. Secondly, we need to be adventurers able to focus and believe that even in the smallest, the most obscure, there's mystery—something fascinating waiting for us to discover. Finally, we must delight in finding significance and connection—not only in the outer world, but also in the world turning inside us.

In these ways, we come into our own, brimming over with whatever struggles life hands us—lost hopes, jobs that didn't pan out, and troubles with our siblings. But also, with life's blessings, the perfection of the night stars, the forgiving circle of friendship, and the beautiful cadence of ever-flowing creativity.

Back to School For Your Inner Artist

*Education is the kindling of a flame, not
the filling of a vessel.*

—Socrates

In those last days of August when you come across a few days of fall-like weather, when the Sunday papers are full of ads for crayons and pens and notebooks, you may feel again the excitement you felt as a child going back to school. Back to school meant new clothes, seeing friends again, and the intoxicating smell of new textbooks. It also meant engaging the brain cells and the prospect of challenging things to learn. For learning is forever, isn't it? Plato said that knowledge is the food of the soul. Life goes on, and our need for nourishment—for learning—does not end. We need to take learning into our *own* hands.

Ask yourself: if you were a master teacher charged with the task of developing a plan of study specifically for your "inner artist" for, let's say, the next three months, what would that plan look like? What do you want and need to learn?

We all have areas of weakness, aspects of our art in which we could grow, and there are various ways of achieving that growth. To broaden in their abilities, visual artists may want to emulate the style of a favorite Old Master, do in-depth work on painting the body, or focus on abstracts. Writers might feel a need to concentrate on plot or character development, or to put an emphasis on creating more writerly magic with imagery. You could also choose more left-brained courses of study, such as improving your skills in technology and learning how to market your work. Or how about a study of yoga for the artist within?

The wonderful thing is that learning something new in one area opens the door to acquiring more expertise in another. And so you grow, develop your skills, and become more and more accomplished as an artist. In addition, it can be a creative activity in itself, developing courses for your curriculum. Try for a good balance—"easy" subjects, intriguing ones, yes, but also those that are going to make you stretch.

Once you've selected a few subject areas, think about the content. Challenge yourself. Remember, you're the master teacher, and you must plan to help your inner artist grow. Develop a reading list relating to your area of study. Set a requirement of a certain number of sunset photographs to complete, or sonnets to write in Shakespearean or Spenserian form. Assign a two-page paper regarding character development, or on varying brushstroke techniques.

By assuming the role of master teacher and creating a plan of study to focus on your own specific needs, you feed your hunger for knowledge, and grow in your area of interest. And besides that, as John Dewey said, "Cease conceiving of education as mere preparation for later life, and make it the full meaning of the present life."[132]

And it's a good life to live.

---

[132] John Dewey, "Self-Realization as the Moral Ideal," *The Philosophical Review* 2, no. 6 (November 1893) 652-664.

Mourning Dove Migration

Art is the act of tuning in and dropping down the well.
—Julia Cameron, *The Artist's Way*

Most of us love autumn, beautiful with its rich colors of red and gold against the emerald of the grass, the burning bushes burning, and the geese filling the skies with their wild cries. Besides marveling in the beauty of the season, we may also experience a sense of sadness—the rhythm of the natural world suggesting all that is about to end.

In late September some years ago, I was driving on the Interstate west to see my parents. Snow Geese flew overhead, and clouds of blackbirds swept up from the sides of the road. I had been thinking about the birds, how we would soon be losing the sights and sounds of them as fall advanced, and remembered an article I'd read in the newspaper about migration—that the mourning doves were some of the first to leave. I turned to my husband in the passenger seat. "Find some paper," I said, "and write this down." And so I wrote a poem, the whole of it seeming to come as a complete piece. Here it is:

Mourning Dove Migration

They're the first to leave,
singly,
or in family groups of two or three
    gone from the rooftops
    gone from the telephone wires
    gone from the puddles at the side of the road
not in noisy symmetry like the Canada Geese
filling the skywith the grandeur of their leaving;

but quietly
in a muffled flutter of feathers
traveling south,
and with them taking
    their plaintive calls at dusk
    their grace
    their meek dark eyes against soft gray.

And it is not until evening, walking
some days or weeks later,
that we look and listen
and wonder
what it is we're missing,
what it is we've lost.

This was the only time I've written a poem this way, the words coming to me out of nowhere. It seemed that all I had to do was to speak them for my husband to write down. How did this happen?

I believe it had something to do with the newspaper article I'd read, the birds overhead, and the fact that I was driving to visit my elderly parents. Also it was autumn, with its little deaths foreshadowing the losses to come. With these thoughts swimming around in my mind, both consciously and below the surface, I was in a state of readiness. And since I was driving, half-absorbed with speed limits and exits and other vehicles around me, my judgmental mind, the small voice that whispers *This is no good; why are you even trying?* was caught off-guard. And the poem came.

Or maybe it was something else. Some unknown entity working through me to help birth the poem into the world. Whatever the reason and however the poem came about, I am grateful. And always I hope for the mystery, the magic, to come again.

When the World is Too Much

The main thing is to be moved, to love, to hope, to tremble, to live.

—Auguste Rodin, *The Origins of Creativity*

"The world is too much with us, late and soon," Wordsworth wrote, "Getting and spending, we lay waste our powers . . ." This was true in 1802 when these lines were first written and it is especially true today. Besides the trouble with "getting and spending," our country is divided, our leadership lacking, and we are besieged by one horrific news story after another. In a world in which so much seems to have gone wrong, how can we cope as individuals? As people trying to live creative lives? We do the best we can, but from time to time we find ourselves becoming detached, anesthetized so as not to feel the pain. This is understandable; but in detaching ourselves from our feelings, we "lay waste our powers."[133] As individuals, we forsake the vibrancy of a rich, full life; and as artists, our creativity slows to a halt.

One of the reasons we detach, I believe, is that we feel helpless. We feel awful about a particular situation but can't see anything we can do about it. Once, after a family argument, I was miserable for two days, unable to do anything but rehash what was said, recognizing my part in the squabble. Then I decided to write a letter. I worded it carefully, expressing my feelings of love and family solidarity, hoping for reconciliation. I took action, and after the letter was posted, I felt better. Later I discovered that the potential rift was mended.

We are responsible people of the world, and we can take action in

---

[133] William Wordsworth, "The World Is Too Much With Us," *Poems, In Two Volumes* (London: Oxford University Press, 1807).

the face of disharmony and ugliness. We can express ourselves and work to create what peace we can. As artists, we do this through our work—lifting our creative voices, and in so doing, making a little space for ourselves to carry on.

In the keynote address at the Nebraska Book Festival in 2014, poet Don Welch spoke of writing taking place in what he called the "tangled bank" of existence, a world confused and mixed up and troubled, a discordant crazy kind of world. What writers can do, he said, is "write in the clearing." Find a place where we can see and make sense of the little part of the world around us.

He also said that in writing, creating, "you feel your way into something, and you 'word' your way out." How wonderful. For isn't this how we write? Create art? Whether we are 'wording' our way to a resolution to the trouble in our midst—or working out chord progressions in a new song, we are seeking a way to understanding, a way to keep going.

Lucy Adkins and Becky Breed

What We've Lost

Every adversity, every failure, every heartache carries within it the seed of an equal or greater benefit.

—Napoleon Hill, *Success Through a
Positive Mental Attitude*

Perhaps you know the story of the young Ernest Hemingway, living in Paris with his wife, Hadley, eking out a living as a news reporter; and in what little extra time he could find, pursuing his passion of writing. In December 1922, he was on assignment in Switzerland, and there he encountered journalist and editor, Lincoln Steffens. The two had met earlier and Steffens had indicated an interest in the young writer's work.

Hadley decided to join her husband (they'd been married only a year), and wanting to surprise him, packed the stories he'd been working on for months, knowing he'd want to show them to Steffens. She boarded the train in Paris, stowed her suitcases, and went back into the station to buy water. When she returned, the small valise with her husband's stories—and the copies she'd included as well—had been stolen. All his work, gone.

A tragic loss. But, as we know, Hemingway went on to write thirteen novels, multiple collections of short stories, a memoir, and won the Nobel Prize for literature.

Camille Pissarro, the Danish-French impressionist painter, suffered a similar tragedy. During the Franco-Prussian War of 1870-71, Pissarro and his family fled to London. When he returned, he found that the Prussians had used his home as a slaughterhouse. In her book, *The Private Lives of the Impressionists*, Sue Roe reported that the soldiers "used Pissarro's canvases, ripped out of their frames, as

247

butcher's aprons and as floor coverings to catch the blood." Although a neighbor managed to save a few, approximately 1,500 paintings were destroyed or gone, "The best part of fifteen years output . . . lost."[134]

How did Hemingway and Pissarro recover from these losses and go on to produce more and better work than they had before? Perhaps it is as Napoleon Hill suggests, that adversity holds the potential for greatness. Or as Henry Rollins writes, "Scar tissue is stronger than regular tissue."[135] In any event, Hemingway and Pissarro were able to find great reserves of strength, and keep on.

Another consideration is the fact that *there was more work for them to do.* Just as the world possesses great abundance in its varieties and numbers of plants and animals, so is the potential for stories to be written, paintings to be painted. The work of creation is limitless. The good news is that the songs we can sing are without number, the beauty we can create without end. In the face of loss, of disappointment or frustration, or whatever situation presents itself to us, there is the opportunity for more. Always we have our work to do.

[134] Sue Roe, *The Private Lives of the Impressionists* (New York: HarperCollins, 2006).

[135] Henry Rollins, qtd. by Gail Blanke, *Becoming.* Web.

For Your Journey

For billions of years, the sun has risen, moved over the curve of earth and then disappeared into darkness. The moon, too, has its cycles, and the earth its seasons. And of course we as creatures of the earth have our seasons of infancy, childhood, adulthood, and ripe old age. We accept these cycles as the natural way of life. But when it comes to dormant times in our creativity, when we go through days or weeks or months of not painting, not writing, not creating, we despair. If we can recognize the fallow times as necessary to our art, as cyclical, we breathe a little easier. We can relax into the quiet time, knowing that more productive days will come.

1. As you are reading these pages, what season is it? Spring, summer, autumn, or winter? *Now, consider where you are in your cycle of creativity. Are you in spring, feeling the sap rising, the first shoots of creativity springing forth? Perhaps you're in summer, a time of exuberance, the work flourishing. Or are you in autumn, bringing a series of paintings to a successful conclusion? Or in winter, experiencing a time of dormancy? Realize that each season has its reason for being, and that the cold of winter is followed inevitably by spring.*

2. We are of the earth and its trees and rocks and meadows, and when we live more closely aligned with the natural world, we experience joy. The heartbeat slows and the mind quickens. We are where we need to be. *Look for ways to spend more time in the out-of-doors. Walk by a creek or river, listen to the rustling of leaves and grasses, take in the changing sights and sounds and smells. Scope out public gardens in your area, parks, wilderness preserves, and other places where you can*

go to re-energize. Plan to visit these places to wander and relax. Take a day to practice your art in the "plein air" as the Impressionist painters did. Write in the out-of-doors—paint or play music. Practice your dance steps under the swaying branches of the willow.

3. Put on some soft music and relax in a comfortable chair. Breathe in a few deep breaths and take a step "outside your-self." Consider yourself from the perspective of a sage teacher watching you with wisdom and kindness.

Then become this sage teacher and devise a three-month curriculum for yourself. Everything is said to be circular, spiral, and for artists, the spiral can go up, up taking you to higher levels of creativity and productivity. As your own mentor/ teacher, you can help yourself to reach these higher levels. What assignments would you give to the "creative you" in progress? If you're a painter, you might assign yourself to study the work of the Blue Riders school or the work of Matisse and try several paintings in that artist's style. If you're a writer of short stories, you might assign yourself to write a story that has the "feel" of a Eudora Welty story. Include in your curriculum 1) books and articles you need to read, 2) field trips you need to take, and 3) assignments you need to complete. Then have some fun with this.

Chapter Twelve:
Just Do It

Make It So

Incredible things can be done simply if we are committed to making them happen.

—Sadhguru, *The Asian Age*

Remember Jean Luc Picard, Starfleet Captain in *Star Trek?* When he and his officers hit upon a solution to get themselves out of a sticky situation—by going to warp speed, say, or activating the deflector shield to evade a hostile force—he instructed his crew to "make it so." And it would be done. I love that. Determining a course of action and following through. Making it so.

Much of what we do in this life is based upon the decisions we make, whether consciously or unconsciously. Generally speaking, if we decide to pursue a particular dream, if we believe in it strongly enough and dedicate ourselves to shepherding it to fruition, more often than not, that dream will come into being. Perhaps you want desperately to achieve a college education. What do you do? Study hard in high school, complete college applications, and line up loans and scholarships. Or perhaps you want to write a novel. You go to work preparing an outline, blocking out periods of time to write, and paragraph-by-paragraph, you write the book. You "make it so."

Decision by decision, we create our lives—committing to relationships, buying condominiums, going on vacations to Hawaii or the mountains. We learn to play the guitar or the piano, create Japan-

251

ese gardens or meditation gardens, convert basement rooms into art studios. When roadblocks appear, circumstances may necessitate we alter our plans somewhat, but when we act on our passions we can create lives which are rich and full, lives full of meaning.

From time to time, however, we may find ourselves feeling stale. Maybe it's time to stretch the imagination, look for ways to further complete our lives. One way we can do this is to set aside time to dream. Get your notebook, number from one to ten, and complete the following phrase: "If all the energies of the universe were with me and I had no fears of failure, I would . . ."

How would you complete the phrase? Maybe you would:

- complete a series of paintings and display them in a local art gallery
- take a pottery class and make vases as gifts for your friends
- begin the novel you've always dreamed of and finish a rough draft in eighteen months

Let your imagination go and jot down as many dreams as you can. Gloria Steinem said that "Without leaps of imagination, or dreaming, we lose the excitement of possibilities. Dreaming, after all, is a form of planning."[136] So let's dream, and allow more possibility into our lives. Then, let's make it so.

---

[136] Gloria Steinem, *Gloria Steinem News*. Web.

Red Purse

Rejoice in small things and they will continue to grow.
—Slaven Vujic, *I see you—A Journey With
Autism: Transformative Memoirs*

When I was a little girl, I was a saver. I was about nine or ten, I think, when I first began to grasp the concept that money was pretty nice to have, that good things were to be had by way of money—things like typewriters and used cars and college educations. Since money was a scarce commodity in my family, I started saving—money from my allowance, dollars given as birthday gifts, any money that came my way. One year, my grandmother gave me a red clutch purse as a Christmas present, and I decided to use this as a bank, saving money from whatever source it came. Time went by, and my red purse grew fatter and fatter. My mother said that if I saved $100 I could open a savings account at the bank. I did, and that account also began to grow.

In my forties I started what I consider serious writing, spending time every day putting pen to paper. I loved poetry, and resolved that in addition to writing all I could, I'd put in more effort editing. When a poem was completed to the best of my ability, I'd enter it in a hardbound journal. How wonderful it was to write in that journal! I had three entries, then four, each time I completed a poem, thinking what a miracle I'd written it. Would I be able to write any more?

So, it was that along with the joy of writing came the fear that I wouldn't be able to repeat my success, wouldn't experience again the heady feeling of creating a poem and finding it halfway good. But I kept on, the poems continued to come, and I filled that journal and started on another. These journals are my "red purses" of poetry, and from time to time, I re-read them, re-experiencing that joy.

The Fire Inside

We all start out as novices following the path to what we love. We are raw material, fresh and untaught. That is a fabulous state to be in, excited and a little nervous, perhaps, but eager to keep on. Looking back on the first poems in my journals, I see that most were a bit simplistic, certainly unsophisticated; but there was also something about them—a certain spark. In my naiveté at the time, I was blind to what was lacking, seeing only that little fire, that spark, and so I kept working happily, writing poem after poem.

For each of us on the path to creativity, it is vital to latch onto that spark—the brilliant moment—hold fast to the thrill of creating, and turn our backs to any deficits in our work. At least at first, until we get our feet firmly planted beneath us. For if we fixate on our shortcomings, compare ourselves to others and come up short, we may become too anxious and fearful and stop creating. If we rejoice in the small things, as Vujic suggests,[137] each new poem or drawing, each new song, we will fill not only our own individual "red purses," but fill ourselves with a sense of satisfaction and pride.

---

[137] Slaven Vujic, *I See You—A Journey With Autism: Transformative Memoirs* (Rebellious Press, 2016).

How Humor Fits In

*If you go with your instincts and keep your humor,
creativity follows.*

—Jimmy Buffett, BookPage Interview

Our creativity is important to us. We take it seriously. But sometimes we take it too seriously, the pressure to create giving rise to such anxiety that all we can think is, *I have to get this done . . . I need a new idea . . . I'm desperate;* and then the playful, imaginative side of us, the side with the best ideas, the most inspired concepts can shut down. We need to lighten up. John Cleese described humor as one of the five most important ways to become more creative. "Humor," he said, "gets us from the closed mode to the open mode quicker than anything else."[138]

Just as stress is the enemy of creativity, humor can be our ally. It takes us out of our routines and offers new perspectives, moves us towards different destinations with unexpected and delightful outcomes. It can break old patterns—the stale and timeworn—and open us to the multiplicities that exist in the world. Humor offers the kind of off-road thinking, divergent brain-storming where imagination can thrive.

Several years ago, I was leader of a group of educators charged with re-organizing an underperforming high school. My instincts told me that humor and play were important in building community, strengthening human connection, and pointing us toward creative solutions. But would it really work? The staff decided to give it a try. We started out telling jokes in staff meetings, sharing quips from

---

[138] John Cleese, *Lecture On Creativity* (1991).

students, and when that seemed to lighten the atmosphere, we took it a little further. First, we invited a comedian to be our speaker for an assembly, and the teachers, seeing how engaged students were, started looking for opportunities to inject humor into their classrooms: sharing funny stories as part of instruction, declaring "Joke Days," and hanging humorous posters. We laughed—a lot—and over time, the mood in the school changed; tensions eased and students shed some of their defenses. In addition, they became more active, not only in learning the basics of math and grammar, but in art, creating stunning textile hangings, pottery, and a mural showing the faces of our multicultural school. Best of all (I think) their writing improved, the storytelling becoming more vivid and imaginative.

Humor can take the form of slapstick, the absurd or ironic; it can be droll, wryly witty, or the kind that makes you double over and wet your pants. Life is difficult at times, and we need a wink, a chuckle, to move us from our dead center positions and get us through. When you're stuck in your art, open your Humor File of favorite jokes, call a friend who makes you laugh, or devise a wickedly funny trick that (in your mind—or not!) you'd like to pull on your office mates.

Mitch Ditkoff said, "It's no accident that *aha!* and *haha* are spelled almost the same way."[139] Loosen up, allow in a little levity, and watch how new possibilities begin to fill your mind. See how the words seem to fly from your pen, how the paint seems to color itself on the canvas. The use of humor helped us make a difference in our school. See what it can do for you.

---

[139] Mitchell Ditkoff. "Great Moments in Creativity." *Idea Champions. Web.*

Ground Blizzard

Art is not a thing, it is a way.

—Elbert Hubbard,
Little Journeys To the Homes of Great Teachers

One March, driving west for a skiing weekend, my husband and I found ourselves in a frightening situation. It was a cold, cloudy day with snow on the ground, but the roads were clear, and we were doing fine until we crossed the Nebraska border into Wyoming. Then the wind began to blow. Fiercely, hard out of the north, and as it blew, it brought snow with it, scudding across our line of vision. The farther west we drove, the more the wind howled, the blowing snow creating a ground blizzard so that visibility extended only a short distance ahead. Luckily, the highway had roadside reflectors about a hundred yards apart, and we spent the rest of the trip, our hearts in our throats, driving past one reflector and waiting the few anxious seconds before the next one came into view.

Sometimes it can feel that way in our creative lives. We start out pursuing our dreams—committing to creative time, finding ways to deepen our abilities, and now and then putting ourselves and our work "out there" for scrutiny. Although we keep doing our jobs as artists, we're not sure we're getting anywhere. That's when we need to keep our eyes open for the "reflectors," those little glimmers that provide hope, that let us know we're still on the road to where we want to go. What are these reflectors? They can be something as simple as an appreciative nod from a mentor or fellow artist, or an invitation to display your photographs in a coffee shop. The occasional acceptance of your poem to a literary journal, or an encouraging note in a rejection letter.

Even better than these outward forms of acknowledgement are the times of inner knowing, arriving sometimes mysteriously. When a small voice inside whispers, *You're getting better, you're getting the hang of it*. That *aha!* moment when you realize you know what to do to make a particular chapter of your novel come alive. These are small moments in a long artistic life, but each is a sign of progress taking us to the next moment and then the next.

E.L. Doctorow said, "writing is like driving a car at night. You can only see as far as your headlights, but you can make the whole trip that way."[140] That's how we live our lives, our artistic lives as well. Driving blind, or nearly blind, depending on the occasional guidepost along the way.

---

[140] E.L. Doctorow, interview by George Plimpton, *The Paris Review* 101 (Winter 1986).

Take a Leap

Pursue what catches your heart, not what catches your eyes.

—Roy T. Bennett, *The Light in the Heart*

The first time I took a leap I was young, about the same age as my fourth-grade granddaughter. So many years ago and I can still remember it, changes churning inside me, subtle, but tangible. It was as if unknown forces had taken camp inside my stomach—driving impulses, fiery urges that kept pushing up like hunger at the end of a long day. What was I longing for?

My school was hosting an art show and I did—no, I *didn't*—want to participate. I was worried. Was I good enough? How could I compare to Robert, who could draw a *real* horse? Or the third grader who did pretty cross-stitch and embroidered a four-colored rainbow? But in art class, we'd been introduced to colored pencils, clay and paint, and a beautiful yearning took hold in me. I loved it, *all* of it, and decided to take the plunge. From that day forward, I formed a new identity, perceiving myself as someone more than the freckle-faced girl who rode a pony and collected rocks. And seeing my lopsided pinch pot in the art show, I felt a warm buzz course from my toes to my head.

Mary Catherine Bateson, author of *Composing a Life*, describes how we as individuals craft our lives from what we are given. She reminds us that, at any age, we can build our lives anew by applying the raw material we already possess, and decide, at last, to use. But we must be willing to take a leap of faith. What does it mean to take a leap of faith? It involves risk-taking, seeing something beautiful on the far side of a chasm and deciding to go for it. Weighing the choice of inaction against the prospect of something dazzling, something truly worthwhile waiting for you. It involves courage, putting yourself out there even if you are afraid of rejection, of failing to meet your own standards, of quitting too early. And it means trusting your gut, knowing that the leap will be worth it, whether or not you entirely succeed.

What makes you pursue a leap of faith? It comes about when you feel a longing, an unanswered call rising inside; and it comes about when a new reality or different art form dangles enticingly in front of you. Then you allow the wonder of your creative instinct to lead you, and you leap, the process of transformation unfolding like a pop-up book, so that you see your words, the paint you work with, the clay, take new form, re-arranging themselves into a short story, a self-portrait, or clay vase. An immense feeling of gratification sweeps over you, and you become aware that you, too, are wonderfully renewed from the inside out.

Reflecting on my personal creative journey, I realize that the times I've ventured out past the breakers have brought me the greatest satisfaction. I've re-crafted my life when I shared a poem with a friend, sent off a manuscript, and, yes, when I entered my pinch pot in the art show.

But first I had to leap.

The Story of Your Art

The most significant creation born of writing is the person the writer becomes for having written.

—Sisters of St. Joseph Carondelet & Consociates
Writer's Circle, *"Tending Writer and Writing"*

This story is your story, a lovely reflection of your life as an artist, how you are given thousands of opportunities to shine through doubt, do your best work, and create art that adds meaning to the world. We want our art to shine like buffed silver, and this requires patience—rethinking, reworking, and polishing, believing in the vision of what could be. It requires faith in what is felt, what is visualized but not yet seen.

For we do visualize it—the script for the play perfected, the photographic image of the locust tree in the dying light of day, the musical score completed so that it reverberates with emotion. But to make the vision a reality, it means going over and over the work until each word, each note is impeccable. It means taking photograph after photograph, failing, and then trying again. Creativity is both a thinking process and an intuitive one. As artists, perhaps the best way to tap into the innate knowledge we possess is to be still for a time—and pay attention to the thoughts running through our heads. We need to know the place we are sitting, and let that inform our work, let art awake in us all the wonder, desire, and sadness we know in our lives, whatever is true and beautiful. And we need to recognize that the insights we receive relate to our lives and experiences.

What is being channeled through you? How can you be the vessel for a work of art, and allow the spirit of inspiration to guide your hands? You must trust in the process of creativity and trust that you are the one to make a specific creation come into being. Maybe you are on fire with a specific societal concern, a certain message you want to share. When you continue working and believing in the mystery, bringing to perfection a vision resonating within, a breakthrough is in the works.

Art-making demands everything from us, but it gives back a hundredfold. Our creative journeys teach us so much—to step out of the way and let transformation work, to abide in the unknowing before certainty occurs, to listen. We must become friends with practice, patience, and resilience; and when our dreams come within grasp, we fall on our knees with gratitude.

On the journey of creativity, our evolution as artists *and* as people might be as important as attaining a particular artistic vision. Before we create art that feeds the soul, we must tend to what is resonating inside. We must be honest about our work, and possess the courage to wander into the unknown. More than anything, we must love deeply, intensely. Love is the heartbeat and sweat of our work, the hot passion for creating.

Pay It Forward

Kindness always leaves a timeless deposit on the heart.

—Molly Friedenfeld,
The Book of Simple Human Truths

What do we do with the paintings we create, the stories we write, the ceramic pots we have piling up in the studio? The art we make is valuable to us. We have a choice as to whether or not we keep it to ourselves or share it with friends and family, at art shows or public readings. Another way to share our work is to pay it forward. *Paying it forward* gives your art, as the French say, *le raison d'etre*—a reason for being—a gift for perpetuity, and best of all, we have the opportunity to enrich another's life.

Why share our art? No matter how we may describe the value of art—art for its own sake or in the opportunities it provides to participate in other realities—one underlying value is that it keeps us from colliding with our everyday selves. What matters are the *encounters* experienced. Whether wrought simply or with great complexity, art helps us discover new passages and confront different viewpoints. It may give us pause. Sometimes we're seized by the recognition of returning to a place we've been before, a place we miss. I experienced such a recognition when my granddaughter Stella gave me a painting she'd created. It was that of a red-tailed hawk rising over the morning sun on beautiful wide-spread wings. The painting was dazzling, and reminded me of a time I once experienced a similar lightness of being, so that momentarily, I was lifted from my everyday world.

When we create, we do so with the idea of being a conduit, to pass along a message or evoke a specific feeling or emotion. We want the readers of our poetry, the viewers of our paintings, to take in and understand our work, value it, and feel an emotional connection—a movement in the chest, a quickening of the heart. But this cannot happen until it is shared. Our attitudes toward what we create can be liberating or stifling. If we put too much pressure on publishing our novels or selling our paintings with an eye on how much money the marketplace will provide in return, art becomes a commodity, something to be bought and sold. And the mystery, the spiritual qualities we have assigned to it, may be lost.

These spiritual qualities are paramount, but we live in a dollars and cents world. There are times we must exchange our art and talents to pay the rent and put food on the table. But there are also times to *pay it forward*. Each of us owes an unimaginable debt to those who have gone before us and paved the way for our creativity, our teachers and mentors, those who believed in us and helped us along—as well as countless others, living and dead, whose work has inspired and informed us. We can't, in any real sense, pay these people *back*, but we can pay it *forward*, using our talents to benefit others.

Many years ago, in a New York subway, my family and I came upon an instance of this: a man standing a little back from the crowd playing his violin, the melody pure and sweet and haunting. We stopped to listen, moved, this beautiful music a gift given freely to all who would listen. Most likely, you are aware of other such examples: visual artists who paint murals in alleyways or in run down neighborhoods for no charge, musicians who provide free concerts at fundraisers. Our art, too, has this potential.

Good art is a life force which is eternal, universal, whether it be Michelangelo's work on the ceiling of the Sistine Chapel or an emotionally-rendered painting of your childhood home. It rejuvenates the soul, gives rise to wonder. Paying it forward opens up the exchange with another, says something about who you are. One creative soul connecting with another.

Going Long, Going Deep

Spiritual love is a position of standing with one hand extended into the universe and one hand extended into the world, and letting ourselves be a conduit for passing energy.

—Christina Baldwin, *Creative Crafting: 52 Brilliant Ideas For Awakening The Artistic Genius Within*

Poet Jim Peterson once shared an epiphany he had: sometimes in conversations we are skipping along on superficialities—the weather—the flu that's going around, and abruptly the conversation takes a turn to something personal, something significant. It's like an energy shift. We switch from the external to the internal, the outward to the spiritual center, and suddenly the air, as Jim explained it, seems "charged with meaning."

Maybe you've experienced this. It happens not only in conversations, but in self-reflection, in relationships, and in our art. Perhaps you are painting, trying to capture the feeling of a friend's kitchen. You paint the yellow and blue wallpaper, the green and red of the potted geranium, all the details of table and chairs, counter and appliances. Then you paint the light fixture above the table, its white light shining down cold and bleak, and suddenly you are overcome with a feeling of profound loneliness. Your friend is a recent widow, and you paint one white plate on the table, one glass and set of tableware, and moisture comes to your eyes. You feel the emotion as you paint, and you see it in the completed work. You've gone from the outside in.

Or it may be that you're working to perfect a dance movement—trying this way and that with a specific gesture or motion, and then something in the particular angle of your arm evokes the tenderness you felt caring for your child when she was ill, three years old and feverish. You feel a shift, and the dance you're working on becomes suffused with a softness and warmth you didn't realize until then had been lacking. It becomes more meaningful, impactful. You have made art.

We come across these moments in every art form, though sometimes we must try another approach, or wait for them to arrive in their own time. As a writer, there are times I go back to review what I have written, a short story or essay which appears fine enough on the surface, but on re-reading seems "flat," so that I'm left wanting more, to come to a new understanding, to feel the stirrings of emotion beneath the words. I try to see these less-than-compelling moments as potential *doors,* places I can expand and search for significance. Then I mark up my paper, drawing little rectangles, *doors,* where I can take the writing to a greater depth. And then I do. All of us can look for these openings—in our writing or singing or acting—and go further into an experience, immerse ourselves. Ask *what really matters here? Is there something I'm avoiding?* Then walk through those doors to a deeper place.

We go long in this creative life, getting up in the wee hours to go to our easels, writing late into the night. And we go deep, trying to discover the crux of the matter, find that "certain feeling" we need in a painting. We do so bringing to bear all that we are, and who and where we come from. We do it, as Baldwin suggests, "with one hand extended in the universe and one hand extended into the world,"[141] finding the energy, the moment "charged with meaning," and passing it along.

---

[141] Christina Baldwin qtd. by Colin Salter, *Creative Crafting: 52 Brilliant Ideas For Awakening The Artistic Genius Within* (Oxford: Infinite Ideas, 2012).

The Power Within

*Incredible change happens in your life when you decide
to take control of what you have power over instead of
craving control over what you don't.*

—Steve Maraboli, *Life, Truth, and Being Free*

Let's say you've been on the creative path for some time, but are feeling depressed, thinking you are not as far down the road as you'd envisioned. You write and you write and you write but the essence of what you want to express remains elusive. Or perhaps you feel that you *have* acquired the chops it takes to be a writer, but your publications remain few and far between. The series of books you dreamed of remains just that—a dream you fear will never be realized.

There are many writers, good and talented, who are dreaming the same dreams you do, wanting validation in the form of publication. The same is true in other areas of creative endeavor—people who are pursuing their aspirations in the visual arts, in photography and acting and design. The competition for public recognition is fierce. The reality is that in some areas of the artistic life, we have little control. We cannot make the publisher publish our book; we have no control over whether the director will choose us for the part in the play. That power lies in other hands.

There is, however, much over which we *do* have control. We can do our work—complete our paintings, learn the new dance routine, write new stories and poems. This is great and joy-filled power. And if publication is your goal, know that every poem you write makes the possibility more likely. Every work you submit makes it likelier still. Rejection has been and will always be a part of the submission process, perhaps because the piece you submit isn't quite "there" yet, or because the editor had a bad day and couldn't see it for what it was. We can't control the latter, but we can continue to hone our abilities—take classes and workshops, strive always for excellence, and keep submitting. We can also take an active part in the artistic community so that when possibilities come along, we will be aware of them. These things we *can* do.

Whether or not we are recognized by the gatekeepers of the art world, our greatest power lies in believing in ourselves and what we are doing. We were born knowing there was magnificence around us; it was magnificence we were created from, and we are capable of greatness we cannot imagine. We are like birds, the ability to sing in our own unique ways embedded within our DNA, the facility of flying in the ways we were meant to fly. We yearn to find the notes to the song, to take wing in flying, and while sometimes we try to suppress that yearning, it is there inside us, waiting like a phone we know is about to ring. And when it does, it will be our destiny on the other end of the line, the call we have been waiting for. All we need to do is answer the phone. Pick up the pen or the paintbrush and do what we were meant to do. Take satisfaction in that, even if the book remains unpublished. "Publication is not all it's cracked up to be," Anne Lamott said. "But writing is."[142]

What matters is the creative act itself—the intense focus, the feeling of reaching beyond yourself to connect with the magnificence of the universe and bring into being some new sort of beauty. There is a sense of fulfillment in that and great happiness; and therein lies true power.

---

[142] Anne Lamott, *Bird by Bird: Some Instructions on Writing and Life* (New York: Pantheon Books, 1994).

Lucy Adkins and Becky Breed

Moments of Truth

My life is my message.

—Mahatma Gandhi,
Mahatma: Life of Gandhi

Although my father was a private person, his beliefs were evident in how he treated the earth, as if it were holy, and in the many ways he applied the wisdom of nature to his life. He didn't just *think* about how he valued the planet, he lived out that basic precept in the activities of each day, his life exemplifying what he believed. Coming from the old school of farming, he recognized that *all* things mattered, that the world consisted of intricate, interwoven elements and he was a vital part of that design.

For over fifty years, Dad worked the land, keeping his family afloat when times were rough. Like many farmers who had to make do, he used his imagination—rigging baling wire, sheet metal, and assorted pipes to repair equipment. Everything was recycled. He figured out how to use parts of an old sundial, re-purposed a leaky bucket into a watering can, a discarded mailbox into a tool shelf. Before it was fashionable, he found inventive ways to collect rain water. His creative mind was evident in the way he designed his fields: the symmetry of the terraces he carved, the fine stitching of yellow threads connecting green quilt blocks of land. Whatever Dad did, he did so appreciating the gift he was given, remaining true to what he saw as his role as caretaker of the earth. My father didn't talk much about what was going on inside him, but sometimes I saw him staring out across the land, taking in the hills, the little grove of trees, the creek, each of the images in his field of vision a moment of truth, an affirmation of the

269

part he played as protector and master craftsman of his small plot of ground.

We all experience moments of truth: intuitive inner feelings, feelings of ecstasy and inner awareness that confirm that we're on the right path—or suggest we need to try something new. But how do we recognize them? A poster for an art exhibit catches your eye and, for whatever reason, you keep thinking about it. Or you view a photography exhibit of wild turkeys in flight and are astonished. *These moments keep showing up.* And you realize that *they are relational*—connected to you in some meaningful way, pulling at you.

Perhaps you read an article about children in Flint, Michigan experiencing the effects of lead poisoning, and realize how directly their plight relates to the children of alcoholics you once taught. You feel a tug in your heart. All children matter. You wonder what you can do. These feelings stick, sweep over you while you're doing the laundry or watching a soccer game, and you know that you need to write, that your printmaking is waiting for you in your artist shed. Your paints are lonely.

You carry within an ancient wisdom that directs you, leads you to a life of fulfillment and promise. And you alone can turn on those moments of truth, transforming them into moments of creativity. Feel the power, the joy, and accept that you, too, are a master craftsman contributing to the beautiful makings of the universe.

For Your Journey

It all seems impossible at times. Our desire to make art, to create the way we know we can when certain conditions are met and the Muse is smiling. We wait until there is a release deep within our bodies, until an emptiness of time and space arrives, until we know what our hands will shape. Yet waiting, waiting for the right moment, the perfect setting, may be the stickler. "Doing" artists, creating artists must be active participants, working in concert with the spirit of the universe and our own deep desires. Be engaged, toil, get your hands dirty, find your sweet spot. This moment is the time to create.

1. This week on your way to work or the grocery, check out all the road signs along the streets or highway. Signs such as: *No Stopping Any Time, Road Closed, Slow Down, Dead End, Passing Allowed, Speed Up. Silently record the ones which resonate with you. When you get to a safe place, write them down. Now reflect on your creativity. Which words describe your creative life today? Which road sign(s) do you want to describe you in the future? Paint, sketch or print the road sign that describes your future creative life.*

2. As an artist, some days you may ask yourself, "How can I create momentum, transform dreaming into action, become right with the universe?" *Let's examine two of the creative tasks in the Torrance Tests of Creative Thinking: 1) Improvement Task. Generate a list of common objects in your home and brainstorm as many ways possible to improve each object; 2) Ask and Guess Task. Select family photos or scenes that convey a story. Formulate possible back stories that lead up to the scene, and several story variations as to what could happen next. Now go*

to whatever art you are working on. What influence does this divergent thinking and problem solving have on your ability to create? Translate into art that which speaks to you.

3. Even when you work and work, establish your routines and follow them, there may come times when you encounter road-blocks, ones you aren't sure you can work your way through. For these difficult times, humor can help. *Watch old episodes of Frazier or Seinfeld or whatever sitcom tickles your funny bone. Google "jokes about writers" and "jokes about artists" and keep a file of your favorites. Let the character in your novel do something silly. Inject a little "joke" into your painting. You might choose to keep the silliness—or not—but a little humor will help you get past the rough spot.*

4. We often celebrate "the firsts" in our lives: the first tooth, the first day at our new job, our first kiss. Yet, we often don't celebrate the firsts associated with what is vital to our quality of life—our creative development. *Maybe you're starting out as an artist and you're a bit hesitant, wanting to talk to a master photographer about focus or lighting techniques, but haven't got the nerve. Claim your "first" by contacting him, beginning a dialogue that may turn into a relationship. Or maybe you're interested in learning how to throw a pot. Claim your "first" by visiting a nearby community college or university art program and ask about classes or workshops you could attend. What will your "firsts" be? Acknowledge and celebrate these. Just do it! You'll be happy you did.*

Sending Forth

You are a person alive with great feeling, a boundless imagination, and potential that has no end. Remember your dreams, and dare to dream new and bigger ones. Let creativity take hold of you and work its magic. Within and without, you are an amazing person, one with a big heart, living and creating in an awesome world, and you can say *yes!* to the adventure that is waiting.

Be patient. Finding your art, your creativity, may take time. But please know that you are not too old, too busy, or too distracted to find what you love and align yourself with that love. The universe is on your side—ideas in the cosmos waiting in limitless numbers, ready to tap you on the shoulder and ask you to bring them into being. Let yourself become still and hear their gentle urging. Then one dream after another, one creative act after another, imagine your life bigger and go about living it.

Living a creative life is part of your DNA, your birthright, bringing with it the gift of a greater awareness of what is around you. It nurtures a deeper love for the world, an appreciation of beauty, and a youthful desire to explore. It makes you more generous and caring, and bestows upon you the resiliency to persevere. We as artists are not broken by the troubles of the world but instead thrive, finding contentment in the creative center we call home.

Find gladness by tapping into the spark that animates you. Create and co-create with others. There will be times when your creativity is dormant, but do not worry. Tomorrow or the next day, you will awake with your senses on fire—a sweet buzz in your head, a quiet heat. It is the life force of creativity, and you are ready for what you are called to do.

References

Anderson, Hans Christian. *The Complete Fairy Tales*. New York: Random House, 1997.

Andrews, Andy. *The Butterfly Effect: How Your Life Matters*. Nashville: Thomas Nelson, 2010.

Angelou, Maya, qtd. by Naomi Epel. *Writers Dreaming: 26 Writers Talk About Their Dreams and the Creative Process*. New York: Vintage Books, 1994.

Atwood, Margaret. "A Progressive Interview With Margaret Atwood" by Matthew Rothschild. *The Progressive*. December 2010.

Baldwin, Christina, qtd. by Colin Salter. *Creative Crafting: 52 Brilliant Ideas For Awakening The Artistic Genius Within*. Oxford: Infinite Ideas, 2012.

Bradbury, Ray, qtd. by Gene Beley. *Ray Bradbury Uncensored! the Unauthorized Biography*. Lincoln: iUniverse, 2006.

Bradbury, Ray. *Zen and the Art of Writing: Releasing the Creative Genius Within You*. New York: Bantam, 1990.

Brandt, Anthony and David Eagleman. "Under the Hood of Creativity," *Time: The Science of Creativity*. August 2018.

Brown, Brene. Interview by Elizabeth Gilbert, "The Way I Share My Soul with the World," *Magic Lessons with Elizabeth Gilbert*. September 30, 2015.

Brown, Greg. "Our Little Town." Track 10 on *One More Kiss Goodnight*. Red House, compact disc.

Bruner, Jerome. *On Knowing: Essays For the Left Hand*. Boston: Belknap Press 1979.

Bryan, Mark and Julia Cameron. *The Artist's Way at Work: Riding The Dragon*. New York: HarperCollins, 1999.

Calacanis, Jason. "7 Voices of Transformation: Interviews with Security Awareness Vendors." O'Reilly.com.

Cameron, Julia. *The Artist's Way*. New York: TarcherPerigee, 1992.

Campbell, Joseph. *The Power of Myth*. New York: Anchor Books, 1988.

Cather, Willa. *Not Under Forty*. New York: Knopf Doubleday Publishing, 1936.

Cather, Willa. *Willa Cather On Writing*. Lincoln: University of Nebraska Press, 1988.

Chesterton, G.K. *Fancies Versus Fads*. New York: Dodd, Mead & Co., 1923.

Cirillo, Francesco. *The Pomodoro Technique: The Life-Changing Time-Management System*. London: Ebury Publishing, 2018.

Cleese, John. *Lecture On Creativity* (1991).

Csikszentmihalyi, Mihaly, qtd. by Geirland, John. "Go With The Flow." *Wired* 4, no. 9 (September 1996).

DeMille, Agnes. *Martha: The Life and Work of Martha Graham*. New York: Random House, 1991.

Dewey, John. "Self-Realization as the Moral Ideal." *The Philosophical Review* 2 no. 6 (November 1893) 652-664.

Dickinson, Emily. "I Dwell in Possibility (466)." *The Poems of Emily Dickinson, Reading Edition*, ed. Ralph W. Franklin (Cambridge: The Belknap Press of Harvard University Press, 1998).

Ditkoff, Mitchell. "Great Moments in Creativity," *Idea Champions*. http://www.ideachampions.com/article_aha.shtml.

Doctorow, E.L., interview by George Plimpton. *The Paris Review* 101 (Winter 1986).

Dylan, Bob, qtd. by Sam Pethers in "June 14th, 1965: Bob Dylan writing 'Like A Rolling Stone,'" *Gaslight Records*. https://gaslightrecords.com/articles/bob-dylan-writing-like-a-rolling-stone.

Earle, Steve. "Pilgrim." Recorded 1998. Track 14 on *The Mountain*. E-Squared, compact disc.

Euland, Brenda. *If You Want to Write: A Book about Art, Independence and Spirit*. New York: Barnes & Noble Press, 2010.

Frost, Robert. Address at Milton Academy. Massachusetts (17 May 1935).

Frost, Robert. "The Road Not Taken." *Mountain Interval*. New York: Henry Holt and Company, 1916.

Gilbert, Elizabeth. *Big Magic: Creative Life Beyond Fear*. New York: Riverhead Books, 2015.

Glaser, Milton, qtd. by Jonah Lehrer. *Imagine: How Creativity Works*. Edinburgh: Canongate Books, 2012.

Goldberg, Natalie. *The True Secret of Writing*. New York: Atria Books, 2013.

Goldberg, Natalie. *Writing Down the Bones: Freeing the Writer Within.* Boston: Shambhala Publications, Inc., 2005.

Greene, Maxine. *Variations on a Blue Guitar: The Lincoln Center Institute Lectures on Aesthetic Education.* New York: Teachers College Press, 2001.

Hardy, Thomas, qtd. by Peter Selgin. *By Cunning & Craft: Sound Advice and Practical Wisdom for Fiction Writers.* New York: F+W Media, 2007.

Heaney, Seamus. "University of North Carolina at Chapel Hill, 1996." In *Take This Advice: The Best Graduation Speeches Ever Given*, 85. New York: Simon & Schuster, 2005.

Hegel, Georg Wilhelm Friedrich and Johannes Hoffmeister. *Lectures on the Philosophy of World History.* Cambridge: Cambridge University Press, 1975.

Hesse, Herman. *Wandering: Notes and Sketches.* New York: Farrar, Straus & Giroux, 1972.

Hikmet, Nâzim. "Things I Didn't Know I Loved." In *Selected Poems of Nâzim Hikmet*, 80. New York: Persea Books, 1975.

Hock, Dee, qtd. by Mitchell Waldrop. "Dee Hock on Management." *Fast Company.* October/November 1996. https://www.fastcompany.com/27454/dee-hock-management.

Huber, Cheri. *How You Do Anything Is How You Do Everything.* Keep It Simple Books, 1998.

James, William. *Principles of Psychology: Volume 1.* New York: Henry Holt & Co., 1918.

Johnsgard, Paul A. *A Chorus of Cranes: The Cranes of North America and the World.* Boulder, CO: University Press of Colorado, 2015.

Kacvinsky, Katie. *Awaken*. New York: Houghton Mifflin Harcourt, 2011.

Karr, Mary. *The Art of Memoir*. New York: Harper Perennial, 2015.

Keats, John. "The Grasshopper and the Cricket." In *Poems*. London: C. & J. Ollier, 1817.

Kellert, Stephen R. "Children, Nature, and the Future of our Species (Giving Children the Gift of Nature)," *Biohabitats* 10, no. 4 (2012): https://www.biohabitats.com/newsletter/giving-children-the-gift-of-nature-2/children-nature-and-the-future-of-our-species-giving-children-the-gift-of-nature/.

Kenyon, Jane. "Mud Season." *Ploughshares* (Summer/Fall 1982).

Kidd, Sue Monk. *The Secret Life of Bees*. New York: Penguin, 2001.

Kidder, Tracy and Richard Todd. *Good Prose*. New York: Random House, 2013, 51.

King, Stephen. *On Writing*. New York: Scribner, 2000.

Kloefkorn, Bill. "#11." *Alvin Turner as Farmer*. Wayne, NE: Logan House Press, 2004.

Kooser, Ted. "Abandoned Farmhouse," *Sure Signs: New and Selected Poems*. Pittsburgh: University of Pittsburgh Press, 1980.

Kooser, Ted. *Winter Morning Walks: One Hundred Postcards to Jim Harrison*. Pittsburgh: Carnegie Mellon University Press, 2000.

Kugler, Jeffrey. "How to Wake Up To Your Creativity." *Time*, April 30, 2017. https://time.com/4737596/sleep-brain-creativity/.

Lamott, Anne. *Bird by Bird: Some Instructions on Writing and Life*. New York: Pantheon Books, 1994.

Lench, Heather, qtd. by Clive Thompson. "How Being Bored Out of Your Mind Makes You More Creative," *Wired* (January 25, 2017).

Lessing, Doris. *The Grass Is Singing.* London: Michael Joseph Ltd., 1950.

Liberman, Nira., Polack, O., Hameiri, B., & Blumenfeld, M. "Priming of Spatial Distance Enhances Children's Creative Performance." *Journal of Experimental Child Psychology* 111, no. 4 (2012): 663-670.

Macy, Joanna; Young Brown, Molly. *Coming Back to Life: Practices to Reconnect Our Lives, Our World.* Gabriola: New Society Publishers, 1988.

Martin, Lee. "Saying Yes," *Lee Martin Author Page*, September 22, 2014. https://leemartinauthor.com/2014/09/22/saying-yes/.

Matheson, Richard, qtd. by Albert J. Parisi. "New Jersey Q & A: Richard Matheson; An Influential Writer Returns to Fantasy." *The New York Times*, April 10, 1994.

Matisse, Henri. "Notes of a Painter," *La Grande Revue* (25 December 1908).

McLean, Don. "Vincent," *American Pie*, United Artist Records, 1971.

Merton, Thomas. *No Man Is an Island.* San Diego: Harcourt & Brace, 2002.

Mickos, Marten, qtd. by Laurence Bradford. "8 Tips For an Amazing Mentor Relationship." *Forbes.* January 31, 2018. https://www.forbes.com/sites/laurencebradford/2018/01/31/8-tips-for-an-amazing-mentor-relationship.

Miller, Henry. *The Rosy Crucifixion I: Sexus.* New York: Grove Atlantic, Inc., 1949.

Munro, Alice. "Dance of the Happy Shades." In *Dance of the Happy Shades* Whitby, Ontario: Ryerson Press, 1968.

Nazarian, Vera, qtd. by Shahira Abdel Shahid. *Roadmap to Success: Inspiring Journeys of Ten Iconic Coptic Leaders*, Bloomington: Archway Publishing, 2016.

O'Connor, Flannery. "Writing Short Stories." In *Mystery and Manners: Occasional Prose*. New York: Farrar, Straus, and Giroux, 1970.

O'Keeffe, Georgia to Alfred Stieglitz. February 1, 1916. qtd. by Judith H. Dobrzynski. "Georgia O'Keeffe's Love Letters: The Steamy Exchange Between O'Keeffe and Stieglitz, Unsealed After 20 Years," *The Daily Beast*, 2009.

Oliver, Mary. "Franz Marc's Blue Horses." In *Blue Horses*. New York: Penguin Books, 2016.

Oliver, Mary. "The Summer Day." In *New and Selected Poems*. Boston: Beacon Press, 1992.

Patawaran, A.A. *Write Here Write Now: Standing at Attention Before My Imaginary Style Dictator*. Mandaluyong: Anvil Publishing, 2016.

Picasso, Pablo, qtd. by Marina Picasso. *Picasso, My Grandfather*. New York: Riverhead Books, 2001.

Pressfield, Steven. *The War of Art: Break Through the Blocks & Win Your Inner Creative Battles*. Black Irish Entertainment, 2002.

Ramsland, Katherine. *Snap: Seizing Your Aha! Moments*. New York: Prometheus Books, 2012.

Reeves, Judy. *Writing Alone, Writing Together*. Novato: New World Library, 2010.

Rilke, Rainer Maria. "Archaic Torso of Apollo." *Ahead of All Parting: Selected Poetry and Prose of Rainer Maria Rilke*, translated by Stephen Mitchell (Modern Library, 1995).

Rilke, Rainer Maria. *Letter Four.* (16 July 1903).

Rilke, Rainer Maria. *Letters To a Young Poet.* New York: W.W. Norton 1993.

Roe, Sue. *The Private Lives of the Impressionists.* New York: Harper-Collins, 2006.

Rollins, Henry, qtd. by Gail Blanke. *Becoming.* http://www.stephen goforth.com/blog-becoming/2015/10/17/worth-fighting-for.

Roshi, Katagiri, qtd. by Marge Hulburt. *Finding Eagle, A Journey Into Modern Day Shamanism.* Missoula: Gone Writing, 2010.

Rosten, Leo, "The Myths by Which We Live," *The Rotarian* 107, no. 3 (1965): 55.

Rousseau, Jean Jacque. *Emile* (1762).

Rumi. "Spring Giddiness," *The Essential Rumi.* San Francisco, CA: Harper, 1996.

Russo, Richard. "Author Richard Russo Ponders What The Presidential Election Was Really About," *Morning Edition.* By Renee Montagne. NPR, November 10, 2016.

Ryun, Jim, qtd. by Nelson, Cordner. *The Jim Ryun Story.* Mountain View, CA: Tafnews Press, 1967.

Sackville, Margaret, qtd. by Susan Ferrier. *The Works of Susan Ferrier.* New York: AMS Press, 1970.

Samuel, Phil and Michael Ohler. "How Manufacturing Managers Can

Tap into the Unlimited Creative Potential of Their Employees." *Industry Week*. October 4, 2012.https://www.industryweek.com/innovation/article/21958563/how-manufacturing-managers-can-tap-into-the-unlimited-creative-potential-of-their-employees.

Schmich, Mary. "Advice, like youth, probably just wasted on the young." *Chicago Tribune*, (Chicago, IL) June 1, 1997.

Schulz, Charles. *It Was a Dark and Stormy Night, Snoopy*. New York: Ballantine Books, 2004.

Sebold, Alice. *The Lovely Bones*. New York: Little, Brown, 2002.

Sexton, Anne. *No Evil Star: Selected Essays, Interviews, and Prose*. Ed. by Steven E. Colburn. (University of Michigan, 1985).

Shapiro, Dani. "On Productive Despair," *DaniShapiro.com* (July 30, 2017).

Shedd, William G.T. qtd. by Gary Ninneman. *C.I.A.: Church in Atrophy*. Maitland, FL: Xulon Press, 2006.

Silko, Leslie Marmon. *Ceremony*. New York: Penguin Books, 1986.

Sontag, Susan. Interview by Edward Hirsch. "Susan Sontag, The Art of Fiction No. 143." *The Paris Review* 137, (Winter 1995).

Stieglitz, Alfred to Sadakichi Hartmann, Apr. 27, 1919. *Alfred Stieglitz/Georgia O'Keeffe Archive, Yale Collection of American Literature*, Beinecke Rare Book and Manuscript Library, Yale University, box 23, folder 546.

Steinem, Gloria. *Gloria Steinem News*. http://www.gloriasteinem.com/news.

Stone, Ruth, qtd. in "Your Elusive Creative Genius," Elizabeth Gilbert. *TED: Ideas Worth Spreading*, 2009. https://www.ted.com/talks/elizabeth_gilbert_your_elusive_creative_genius.

Strayed, Cheryl. *Wild: From Lost to Found on the Pacific Crest Trail*. New York: Alfred A. Knopf, 2012.

Ueland, Brenda. *If You Want To Write*. Minneapolis: Graywolf Press, 1997.

Walsch, Neale Donald. *Conversations With God*. New York: Penguin Putnam Inc., 1995.

Warhol, Andy. *The Philosophy of Andy Warhol (From A To B & Back Again)*. San Diego: Harcourt Brace Jovanovich, 1975.

Watterson, Bill. *The Essential Calvin and Hobbes: A Calvin and Hobbes Treasury*. Kansas City: Andrews McMeel Publishing, 1988.

Weinbaum, Dave. "The secret to a rich life is to have more beginnings than endings," *Jewish World Review* (July 14, 2017). http://www.jewishworldreview.com/dave/weinbaum071417.php3.

Wheatley, Margaret and Myron Kellner-Rogers. "The Promise and Paradox of Community." *The Community of the Future*. Jossey-Bass, 1998.

Whitman, Walt. "Song of Myself." *Leaves of Grass*. New York: Doubleday Publishing, 1855.

Whyte, David. *Consolations: The Solace, Nourishment and Underlying Meaning of Everyday Words*. Langley, WA: Many Rivers Press, 2015.

Williams, Tony. "The Writer Walking the Dog: Creative Writing Practice and Everyday Life." *American, British, and Canadian Studies* 20, no. 1 (2012): 224-238.

Winfrey, Oprah, qtd. by Caroline Castrillon in "5 Steps To Turn

Passion Into Profit," *Forbes* (March 8, 2020). https://www.forbes.com/sites/carolinecastrillon/2020/03/08/5-steps-to-turn-passion-into-profit/#29e9cc3c700b.

Woolf, Virginia. *The Diary of Virginia Woolf: Vol. IV, 1931-35*. Edited by Anne Oliver Bell and Andrew McNeillie. London: Hogarth, 1982.

Wordsworth, William. "Ode: Intimations of Immortality from Recollections of Early Childhood," *Poems, in Two Volumes*, (London: Longman, Hurst, Rees, and Orms. 1807).

Wordsworth, William. "The World Is Too Much With Us." *Poems, In Two Volumes*. London: Oxford University Press, 1807.

Valery, Paul, qtd. by Timothy Ferris. *The Coming of Age in the Milky Way*. New York: HarperCollins, 2003.

Van Gogh, Vincent. Letter to Theo van Gogh, 16 October 1888.

Vujic, Slaven. *I See You—A Journey With Autism: Transformative Memoirs* (Rebellious Press, 2016).

Young, Julian. *Friedrich Nietzsche: A Philosophical Biography*. (Cambridge University Press, March 8, 2010).

Zander, Rosamund and Benjamin. *The Art of Possibility*. New York: Penguin Books, 2002.

Zwerling, Lynn. "Knitting Behind Bars, Learning Focus And Patience," *Tell Me More*, NPR (January 9, 2012).

Acknowledgements

We would like to express our deep gratitude to the many people who inspired and encouraged us over the years: our mentors and friends who believed in us and helped us keep the faith. Thank you to those who shared their stories, to the students in our workshops whose work stirred us and compelled us to keep going, and to our fellow writers whose companionship and understanding we could not have done without.

Many thanks go to early readers Dr. Teresa Abrahams and Claudia Reinhardt, and particularly to Erin Littlewood whose close reading and thoughtful support pointed us in the right direction. We'd also like to express special thanks to Pam Barger for her confidence in this work, her insights, and her editorial assistance.

Thank you to Terri Ann Leidich and the fine people at WriteLife Publishing for trusting in this book and helping to bring it into the world; and lastly to Tom and Gale for their willingness to listen and for believing in us.

About the Authors

Lucy Adkins earned her MFA from the University of Nebraska at Omaha and is a writer of poetry, fiction, and nonfiction. Her poetry and short fiction have appeared in many journals and anthologies, and her first poetry chapbook, *One Life Shining*, was published by Pudding House Press. She co-presents the Nebraska Humanities program "Diaries and Letters of Early Nebraska Settlers," and is a frequent writing instructor for OLLI, Osher Lifelong Learning Institute, and the Larksong Writers' Workshops. Her book, *Two-Toned Dress*, was the winner of the 2019 Blue Light Press poetry chapbook contest.

Becky Breed, a veteran educator, poet, and essayist, co-wrote and facilitated "Women at the Springs," a Nebraska Humanities program empowering women to live more courageously, as well as "The Intergenerational Project" connecting elders and teens through stories to promote communication, writing, and use of the media. She has an Ed.D. in Education, and in addition to teaching at the university level, was the principal of a Gold Star School which was awarded recognition for significant improvements in reading, writing, and math. The students' resiliency and drive to be the best they can be helped shape the fabric for several of the enclosed essays.

Together the two co-authored *Writing in Community: Say Goodbye to Writer's Block and Transform Your Life*, which was awarded an "IPPY" in the Independent Publisher Book Awards. *Writing in Community*, the first book in their "Essential Writing and Creativity" series, along with the impact of Adkins' and Breed's many presentations and workshops led to their being named winners of the 2020 Lincoln, Nebraska Mayor's Arts Award in Artistic Achievement in Literature.

Volume 1 of The Essential Writing and Creativity series

Writing in Community is a book of inspiration and encouragement for writers who want to reach deep within themselves and write to their fullest potential. There is magic in a successful writing group. This book helps writers tap into that magic, and with gentle wisdom and humor, experience unprecedented breakthroughs in creativity.